THESE TEN WORDS

These Ten Words

Roy L. Honeycutt, Jr.

BROADMAN PRESS
Nashville, Tennessee

For
my son Roy Lee, III

© 1966 · BROADMAN PRESS
All rights reserved
Third Printing

4212-09

ISBN: 0-8054-1209-3

Scripture quotations are for the most part
from the Revised Standard Version.

DEWEY DECIMAL CLASSIFICATION NUMBER: 222.16
Library of Congress catalog card number: 66-15530
Printed in the United States of America

CONTENTS

Introduction....7

1. Priority....16

2. Sovereignty....29

3. Sincerity....40

4. Sanctity....49

5. Unity....60

6. Responsibility....70

7. Fidelity....82

8. Honesty....94

9. Integrity....103

10. Security....115

Bibliography....126

INTRODUCTION

We never outgrow the Ten Commandments because we never outgrow God. Despite our sophisticated pretensions toward self-sufficiency, each of us knows his own desire for the comforting reality of God's presence. Whatever the reason for our frequent indifference to him, deep within we hear the continual voice which reminds us that we need him. Each of us longs to rise above life's swirling and conflicting clouds into his realm of life.

The Ten Commandments are among those biblical mountain peaks that thrust themselves beyond the clouds into the very presence of God. Those who are willing to scale the ascending slope of Sinai are assured that God will meet them there, speaking once again to those who listen with ears of faith. He will not only make the journey with us, however, but at the end of the way our communion will be deeper, his reality more captivating than ever before. Like Jacob's ladder (cf. Gen. 28:10 ff.), the Commandments bear two-way traffic between earth and heaven. With its bottom resting in our human predicament and its top planted securely against the bulwark of God's compassionate involvement in our situation, this ladder lifts men to the heights of God's loving presence.

On one occasion, as I sought to give written expression to the relevance of the Commandments, I wrote, "The Ten Commandments are as relevant to your life as God himself." Yet, better judgment soon prevailed and this was altered. I had mistakenly equated the essence of God with one expression, one witness, of his nature. God and the Commandments are not synonymous, despite the close interrelationship of the written Law and the lawgiver. We should never equate God with any expression of his essence (this is merely another form of idolatry!). Despite the fact that the Bible is the written Word of God, not even the Scriptures should be confused with God. God always stands above and beyond any given witness, written or otherwise. So, while the Commandments are legitimate witnesses to God, they should remain just that. They are witnesses.

Because the Commandments are witnesses to God, however, there is a sense in which their relevance and the relevance of God are so intertwined as to be almost inseparable. Consequently, if God is relevant for your life, the Commandments will also be deeply relevant. For they are the written expression of God's character and demand.

Law and Covenant

The Ten Commandments are addressed to a redeemed people, the covenant community. The preface declares with finality: "I am the LORD your God, who brought you out of the land of Egypt, out of the house of bondage" (Ex. 20:2).

The name LORD, or more properly *Yahweh* (rather than the older *Jehovah*), was the name of the covenant God (cf. Ex. 3:14; 6:3). Its use compares with the practice of addressing someone today by his first name. To use the name LORD, therefore, implies (1) the redemptive activity of God (for the LORD was the God who redeemed Israel from Egypt), and (2) personal acquaintance with God within the covenant, for the name LORD (Yahweh) is never used except in the context of the covenant community.

The Commandments are addressed to a people whom God has redeemed and with whom he has entered into covenant. Rather than expressing the demand of God for all humanity, they represent the insistent voice of God calling to those who have been redeemed by his mighty hand and outstretched arm from the bondage of their Egypt—whether ancient or modern.

Some would so universalize the Commandments as to ignore the specific relationship between their demand and the redemptive activity of God. The most extreme example of this broad view of the Commandments may be seen in the efforts of one writer to demonstrate that even animals live within the boundary of the principles of the Ten Commandments.[1] Others see the Commandments as the embodiment of principles that are operative in all human existence, apart from the redeemed community. There is an element of truth in the latter assertion. Those who murder, steal, commit adultery, or violate any of the Commandments set themselves against the seemingly immovable forces of retribution present in the moral order. Yet, this does not come to grips with the biblical understanding of the Commandments.

Biblically understood, the Commandments represent the demand of God for his Chosen People. Those demands at times coincided with other legal or moral codes of the ancient Near East. Consequently, for Israel the uniqueness of the Commandments lay not in terms of universal moral principles but in the awareness that they were the rightful expectation of her LORD; an expectation grounded in his redemptive activity.

The relationship between covenant and law in the ancient Near East is a commonly accepted principle in contemporary Old Testament studies. George Mendenhall has unmistakably illustrated this close relationship in his work *Law and Covenant in Israel and the Ancient Near East*. There is adequate historical and archaeological evidence for support of the thesis that the Commandments are addressed to a redeemed people; that they are to be understood in light of the common union of law and covenant in the ancient Near East.

By what reason, therefore, should we today anticipate that men who have not known the redeeming power of God should maintain the Ten Commandments? Apart from a new heart and a new spirit, is it possible for unredeemed men to live by the demands of the redeemed community?

Both the Ten Commandments and the Sermon on the Mount are addressed to members of the covenant community. While men are to be commended in setting these high biblical patterns as their ideal, this is not the point of beginning. The point of beginning is an experience with the redeeming LORD.

It is not to be implied that men outside the covenant community are free from divine responsibility nor that their actions are excusable. There are media of natural revelation (cf. Rom. 1:18 ff.), and some aspects of special revelation also involve all men.

Name, or Terminology

While the demands of God (cf. Ex. 20:2 ff. and Deut. 5:6 ff.) are popularly known as "the Ten Commandments," they are never so referred to in the Hebrew Bible. First, both Deuteronomy and Exodus refer to them as the *ten words*, although English translations use "commandments." This may be because of modern familiarity with the term (cf. Deut. 4:13; 10:4; Ex. 34:28). The Greek translation of the Old Testament, the Septuagint, translated Deuteronomy 10:4 as *deka logous* or "ten words." This eventually gave rise to the designation of the Ten Commandments as the "decalogue." The term "decalogue" is therefore more nearly correct than the "ten commandments."

Second, the Commandments are also referred to in the Old Testament as *"the testimony"* (cf. Ex. 25:16). The reference intended to convey the idea that the "ten words" were testimonies to the will of God.

Finally, the Commandments are referred to in the Old Testament as *"the covenant"* (Ex. 34:28; Deut. 4:13; 9:9). This designation probably arose out of the close relationship between the Commandments and the covenantal responsibilities of the people. They so summarized the demand of God that they could be spoken of as "his covenant" (Deut. 4:13) or "the tables of the covenant" (Deut. 9:9).

What does the present author mean by the title THESE TEN WORDS? Simply that the "word" aspect of the Commandments more nearly captures the essence of their meaning. Obviously, the original writer did not mean ten literal words. There is no possible way whereby the Commandments could ever have been reduced in Hebrew to ten actual words.

To understand what the writer sought to convey, it is necessary to recognize that a word, even in contemporary understanding, is simply a means of communicating a concept or an idea. We see an object with four legs, a seat, and a back. We call it a chair. In speaking the word "chair" we have communicated a concept more complex than a single word. Again, the word "missile" conveys an all but innumerable series of meanings or concepts to the mind. The word itself is subordinate to the idea which we seek to convey. For example, when we forget the name of an object often we coin a word to convey the idea. Forgetting the name "clamp," "wrench," and so on, someone says, "Hand me that thingamajig," or that "whatcha-ma-call-it." Highly colloquial —yes—but also highly expressive. In itself the word had no meaning, yet it had the power to communicate meaning. Words are no more than vehicles that have emerged to transport the concepts, ideas, or feelings we wish to express.

The "ten words" are therefore ten disclosures of the will of God—ten concepts, or ten principles which the covenant people are to embody in their life before both God and man. In this study, let us look for ten principles, or ten self-disclosures of God's will.

Beyond the words, we should *seek* the LORD. If we do this, then the Commandments will have much to say to us today, for principles do not change. While applications may have to be reshaped according to the demands of different generations, the ten words, or ten concepts, given by God are as changeless as the will and purpose of the God who gave them.

Division of the Commandments

Within Judaism, the verse beginning, "I am the LORD thy God" is taken as the First Commandment. The redemptive activity of God was felt to have been so important that this prefatory statement was actually made the First Commandment. To maintain the number "ten" for the total number of Commandments, the First and Second Commandments (according to our own division) were combined and considered as the Second Commandment.

Another division is found in the Roman and Lutheran churches who, following the example of Augustine, merge the First and Second Commandments into a single commandment, considering the combination as the First Commandment. In order to preserve the total number of ten, what we know as the Tenth Commandment was divided, thus making their Ninth and Tenth Commandments.

How is one to arrive at a correct division of the Commandments?

First, the Commandments are generally recognized to have been stated primarily in negative form. In Hebrew, the form *lo'* precedes negative assertions. Using this as a guide, it seems fairly clear that phrases beginning with the negative form (e.g., our First and Second Commandments) are separate commandments. Second, considering the Roman approach, why would the writer specify "Thou shalt not covet thy neighbour's wife" (their Ninth Commandment), when the Seventh Commandment had already dealt with adultery? What we know as the Tenth Commandment deals with covetousness, nothing else. Hence, it is improper to divide it so that half of verse 10 deals with coveting a wife and half with property, for in Old Testament times the wife was considered together with other property a man owned.

The division with which we are most generally familiar is likely the correct one. At least it was recognized by ancient Jewish writers, Philo and Josephus, Origen and the early Christian church, the later Greek church, and the Reformed churches generally.

Value of Negative Form

Now and then one hears the objection that because of their strongly negative character the Ten Commandments are not in the spirit of the Christian faith. Is there value in the negative form?

First, in their original setting, the negative form may be viewed as having allowed greater lattitude to the nomadic tribesmen, accustomed to freedom, than a series of positive injunctions. As Mendenhall observes: "It has been pointed out that prohibitions only are universal, since they define only the areas which are not permitted, *leaving all other realms of action free*. A positive command, on the other hand, immediately excludes all other alternatives." [2] By thus leaving all other action to the self-determination of the people, under the spirit of the covenant, the Commandments actually assured for Israel a degree of freedom which is seldom observed.

Second, in answer to the criticism that the Commandments are "too negative," would anyone actually maintain that there is no place for prohibitions in society? Are we so positive in our thought as to believe that we must never say no—and sometimes quite loudly? By what stretch of the imagination could one object to a commandment that prohibits theft or adultery? Can you visualize a community in which theft, murder, adultery, dishonesty, and covetousness were allowed to reign with never a word to discourage their practice? After all, man is not God to say what is to be yes or what is to be no!

God's Continuing Word

The Ten Commandments are not always recognized as relevant for the Christian life. This stems, in large measure, from two sources.

First, there are those who miss the relevance of the Commandments because they do not recognize that the ten concepts which God revealed were given through the modes of thought and cultural patterns of the day. Many ancient customs have altered, but this does not mean that the spirit which prompted the Commandments should be abandoned. As a consequence of this attitude an Anglican minister dropped the Commandments from his church services, because "they are not Christian."[3] The Second, Fourth, and Tenth Commandments, he said, did not apply in the modern world. How tragic it is that this minister never learned from a study of biblical criticism that while the particular form of the Scriptures may be outdated (for example, viewing one's wife as a piece of property), the content abides. Surely no one would assume that the Tenth Commandment teaches such a permanent position for woman. At the same time, no one—or, so it would seem—would cast out a prohibition against covetousness, the root of so much of the restless dissatisfaction and open strife in our midst today.

Second, some miss the relevance of the Commandments because they never understand that the Bible deals in principles applicable to every age. An examination of Jesus' treatment of the Commandments in the Sermon on the Mount illustrates the manner in which the spirit of the Commandments must be lifted out and applied to new situations of a given generation. Jesus was not content with the statement that man should not murder. He saw that the principle behind the Fifth Commandment dealt with one's respect for the personality of another (cf. Matt. 5:21 ff.).

In our own generation the Bible will speak to us when we (1) recognize that while the human form in which the Scriptures came may change from one era to another, the divine content of its message never does, and when we (2) seek to find the principle which gave birth to a commandment or biblical statement, and then apply that spirit to the involvements of our own generation. In this manner the Commandments, the entire Bible, will speak to us with relevance and divine authority.

Unless we follow some such practice, however, we may find ourselves studying what God once said to Israel and never realize that God is trying to break through into our modern situation and apply the same principle to us. Throughout the present book the deliberate effort will be made to strip away the ancient Near Eastern form in which the Commandments came; then to reclothe the kernel of divine truth in modern form. That this is a hazardous task, I fully recognize. But unless we do this, we will never take the words of God, spoken so long ago, and make them relevant to our own life situation.

Notes

1. See Ernest Thompson Seton, *The Natural History of the Ten Commandments* (New York: Charles Scribner's Sons, 1907).

2. George E. Mendenhall, *Law and Covenant in the Ancient Near East* (Pittsburgh: The Biblical Colloquium, n.d.), p. 7. Italics are mine.

3. George Wilkins, in *Kansas City Times*, October 17, 1960.

I
PRIORITY

"Who is your god?" Or, in our age of extreme materialism, perhaps it would be better to ask, "*What* is your god?"

"I don't have a god—I can't believe," some would answer. Yet, is this possible? Has there ever been a person who lived without a god? Oh, you may not call him a god. You may not know his name. But he is there. Martin Luther once raised the question, "What means it to have a god?" and then answered, "Whatever thy heart clings to and relies upon, that is properly thy god."

The First Commandment says, "Thou shalt have no other gods before me" (Ex. 20:3).

If you would dare test your own commitment, the absolute loyalty of your life, then ask this question, "What are the real driving forces of my actions when I am free to act as I wish?" The answer which you give will indicate with startling clarity the gods you really worship. "You belong to the power which you choose to obey" (Rom. 6:15).[1]

Even those who disclaim faith in the LORD have a certain inclination toward him in their more serious moments. For example, it is reported by one who knew the daughter of Karl Marx that on an occasion when the conversation turned to religion, she said, "I was brought up without any religion. I do not believe in God." Then she added a bit wistfully, "But the other day in an old German book I came across a German prayer and if the God of that prayer exists, I think I could believe in Him." When asked what the prayer was, the reply came slowly in German, "Our Father, which art in heaven." [2]

Atheism has never been our real problem. "In every instance," says J. H. Oldham, "there is in the last resort something on which a man depends and to which he gives his final allegiance.... When God has been slain men find themselves driven to put something in His place, some object in which they can place their final trust, some idol of their own making." [3] The question is not whether we believe but in whom or what we believe.

The First Commandment takes religious commitment for granted. It assumes that men will give their loyalty to a god, or gods. This is never argued. Therefore, the central thrust of the First Commandment can be summed up in one word—PRIORITY. Of all possible loyalties a man can have, which is to have priority?

One or Many Gods?

Ancient Near East religion.—Atheism was unheard of in the ancient Near East. Just as the Bible never sought to prove the existence of God, neither did ancient Near Eastern cultures question the reality of their gods. Indeed, gods abounded on every hand—gods of sky above and earth below; gods of the mountains, streams, and fields; gods that blessed and gods that cursed; gods of the sea and gods of the soil.

The gods stood behind the phenomena of the world. For example, the wonderful qualities of the reed marshes in Mesopotamia which could produce a shepherd's pipe for music, or a scribe's pen for writing, were attributed to the goddess Nidaba. It was Nidaba who made the reeds thrive. If she were not present the shepherd could not produce his music. The scribe attributed to her the difficult piece of writing which came from his stylus.

It was also generally agreed in the ancient world that every nation had its own god, or gods. Each god was limited to the land of his particular nation. The best example of this emerges in the rather strange request that Naaman made to Elisha (cf. 2 Kings 5:15 ff.). After Elisha had healed the Syrian commander, Naaman asked that he be given "two mules' burden of earth; for henceforth your servant will not offer burnt offering or sacrifice to any god but the Lord" (v. 17, RSV). Naaman had come to believe that there was "no God in all the earth but in Israel" (v. 15). Yet, in order for him to worship the Lord in Damascus it was necessary, according to his understanding, to transport some of the land of Israel back to his own home so that he could worship the Lord.

The identification of the gods with particular nations was also reflected throughout the history of Israel in the concept that the conflicts of Israel with other nations were actually conflicts of her God with those nations, and perhaps with the gods of those peoples. This was especially revealed in the Egyptian crisis at the time of the Exodus, the conquest narratives, the Assyrian crisis of the eighth century, and the encounter of the Lord with the powers of Babylon during the exile.

Israel and other gods.—The Old Testament reveals that Israel often spoke of other gods. Deuteronomy, for example, deals at length with the inherent danger of abandoning the Lord in order to follow the gods of the new land into which Israel was entering (cf. Deut. 12:29 f.; 13:1 ff.; 29:25 ff.; 30:17 f.). In a covenant renewal ceremony in the valley of Shechem, Joshua challenged his people to devotion to the Lord: "Put away the gods which your fathers served beyond the River and in Egypt, and serve the Lord. And if you be unwilling to serve the Lord, choose this day whom you will serve, whether the gods your fathers served in the region beyond the River, or the gods of the Amorites in whose land you dwell; but as for me and my house, we will serve the Lord" (Josh. 24:14–15). Jephthah later addressed the Ammonites in such manner as to reflect the common belief in multiple gods: "Will you not possess what Chemosh your god gives you to possess? And all that the LORD our God has dispossessed before us, we will possess" (Judg. 11:24). The bitterest aspect of David's exile to the land of the Philistines was, according to his own statement, the fact that "they have driven me out this day that I should have no share in the heritage of the LORD, saying, 'Go serve other gods'" (1 Sam. 26:19, RSV). Ludwig Köhler notes that "These 'other gods' are mentioned 63 times."[4] In all of this, early Israel shared the common view of the day concerning the domain of one's God. Moab and Ammon had their gods. Israel had her God.

Many have understood the First Commandment as a statement of monotheism, the belief in only one God. Yet, this is not as clear as some would assume. The commandment insists that there be no other gods *before* the LORD (literally "upon, or over, against my face"; i.e., in preference to me). This does not mean that the commandment takes a permissive attitude toward the gods of other nations. Neither does it mean that the commandment passes judgment on the reality of the gods of other nations; whether or not they actually exist, other than as a projection of man's understanding. The main thrust of the commandment centers in the fact that *for Israel* there is to be no other God. Priority is to be given to the LORD who redeemed them from Egypt.

In suggesting that priority be given to the LORD, however, one should not conclude that Israel could worship other gods so long as these gods were kept in a position subordinate to the LORD. The commandment, in effect, passes over the gods of other nations in silence, and comes to the point of true significance in its insistence that Israel shall worship no other gods.

Israel's belief in only one God.—Did Israel ever arrive at the point of insisting that not only was she to serve the one LORD but that no other gods actually existed? Isaiah, Hosea, Amos, Micah, great prophets of the eighth century, and no doubt others, did recognize that they not only were to worship no other gods before the Lord but that *there are no other gods* but the Lord! Jeremiah's ridicule of the idols of his day leaves little question concerning his own conviction that the Lord alone existed as God (cf. Jer. 2:26 ff.; 10:1 ff.). It is in the exilic portions of Isaiah that the strongest statement on monotheism in the Old Testament is made. "I am the Lord, and there is no other" (45:5), says the Redeemer of Israel. "Before me no god was formed, nor shall there be any after me" (Isa. 43:10; cf. Isa. 41:28 f.; 42:17; 44:7 f. 45:16; 46:1 f.). Deuteronomy also insisted on the uniqueness of the Lord: "The Lord is God; there is no other besides him" (4:35).

In the course of his continuing revelation, Israel did come to see with unmistakable clarity that there were no other gods. The end of God's purpose was not clear from the beginning, but she slowly came to apprehend that not only should she serve the Lord alone but that he alone actually existed.

Progressive apprehension of the will of God.—Involved in all that has been said is the principle of progressive apprehension of the will and nature of God. The Old Testament revelation came in terms and modes of thought which could be apprehended in a particular era. How else could God work with a people other than where they were in their understanding at a given point? God took Israel where he found her, and as he revealed his will she progressively apprehended his purposes. The fulness of his revelation did not come for a thousand years or more, when the appearance of his Son perfectly embodied the will of the Father. In all of that intervening time God was working with his people, molding and shaping their understanding to the end that ultimately they would apprehend that which he had intended all along.

Some have applied the term "progressive revelation" to the process by which Israel came to understand more clearly God's nature and will. It could more accurately be described as progressive apprehension. God always stood ready to reveal himself fully. Man, not God, was the limiting factor. The people simply could not apprehend, initially, the full impact of God's total revelation. They were as children, who must be led step by step, precept by precept, toward the full understanding the parent desires for them.

Such an understanding of the revelation of God will do much to clarify many of the moral problems of the Old Testament: polygamy, vindictive destruction of enemies (cf. Psalm 137:1 ff.), and generally sub-Christian action. These were not always the absolute will of God. Often they were the shadowed understanding of ancient man.

Such a concept will also do much to explain the First Commandment. In commanding Israel to worship "no other gods," the LORD was beginning with Israel where she was in her understanding of God—the acceptance of many gods. Thus, Israel received an understanding of practical monotheism in that *for her* there was no other god. Theoretical monotheism waited for the continued unfolding of the will of God, however, and in the interval Israel continued to struggle with the temptation to follow other gods.

The Priority of the LORD *for Israel*

The priority of God's claim upon the loyalty of Israel was grounded in the redemptive activity of the LORD. Because he had redeemed her from the bondage of Egypt, he had every right to speak with a note of authority. The point of beginning for Israel always centered in the Exodus experience. Although the creation narratives appear first in the Bible, this does not mean that creation was first in the thought of Israel. The theological point of beginning for Israel lay in the redemptive activity of the LORD. Israel did not begin with creation and reason from that point to the sovereignty of the LORD. Rather, Israel began with the redemption of the LORD and his subsequent sovereignty. She then reasoned that if the Lord redeemed surely he must also have created.

Israel's response to the command of the Lord was not grounded in abject fear; rather, it was grounded in love and grace. Because of what God had done for her she was to keep his commandment. Such response was much akin to the later words of our Lord, "If you love me, you will keep my commandments" (John 14:15). As George Ernest Wright has suggested, "Israel conceived of the law not as a penal burden to be borne but as a special gift of God, that a people who had been without law might now have it and in it find justice and security." [5]

Biblical insistence upon the priority of the Lord is heard with clarity throughout both Testaments. In the beginning it appears in the temptation experience of Genesis 3:1 ff. Who is to have priority—the Lord or man? It continues in the patriarchal narratives—in the tension between faith and lack of faith in the life of Abraham and in Jacob's opposite poles of rascality and saintliness. Moses responded to the apostasy of Israel under Aaron by calling upon those who were on the Lord's side to stand on one side of a line drawn in the desert sands of Sinai. In his covenant renewal ceremony Joshua called for the absolute priority of the Lord over all other gods. Elijah later echoed the same thought, "If the Lord is God, follow him; but if Baal, then follow him" (1 Kings 18:21, RSV.). Hosea sought to correct Israel's mistaken ascription of life's blessings to Baal (cf. 2:8); The Lord was their "God from the land of Egypt; you know no God but me, and besides me there is no savior" (Hos. 13:4, RSV).

The New Testament is quite clear in calling for the priority of the Lord. Jesus himself said that no man could serve two masters (cf. Matt. 6:24). Later, he insisted that those who were not for him were against him (cf. Matt. 12:30). Those have chosen that better part in life who give themselves to his service, he pointed out in the face of Martha's complaining spirit (cf. Luke

10:38 ff.). No man having put his hand to the plow and looking back is fit for the kingdom of God (cf. Luke 9:62), and no manner of desire for the gifts of the kingdom could be substituted for the renunciation of all in order to follow him (cf. Matt. 19:16 ff.). His true mother and brothers were not of the flesh but "those who hear the word of God and do it" (Luke 8:21, RSV). In his basic call to discipleship Jesus insisted that those who seek to save their lives would inevitably lose them; that only those who are willing to lose their lives in his service would find them (cf. Matt. 16:25).

Yet, renunciation was of no value within itself. Its value appeared only when it was practiced in order to manifest faithfulness to the priority of the Lord. Whatever might interfere with that greater loyalty to the Lord must be sublimated to the higher interests of his kingdom. Surrender must always be for the sake of a larger good, never an end within itself. Renunciation is, therefore, the logical corollary to the priority of God. By denying himself, a man becomes capable of the service of God, and only in this service can he truly fulfil himself.

The Priority of the Lord *Today*

What does the First Commandment have to say to us today? Are we to dismiss the commandment as an outdated relic of the past, when men believed in many gods? Should we regard it as no more than the expression of an extreme and narrow nationalism, seeking to advance the interests of its own god? Or, perhaps, should the commandment be studied as one facet in the unfolding revelation of God to Israel but of no consequence to those who are committed to the Christian faith today? Regardless of its cherished position in the traditions of Judaism and Christendom alike, is this commandment relevant to life in the twentieth century? This is the crux of the entire issue!

Modern threats to the Lord.—To speak of "modern threats to the Lord" could lead to misunderstanding. Obviously, in one sense God himself is never actually threatened. It is rather our own loyalty to him that is threatened. Yet, in the sense that our loyalty or priority concerning God is threatened, God is also threatened. What are some of the modern threats to the Lord?

First, *individualism* constitutes a serious threat to the priority of the Lord. Ours is a generation in which freedom has been perverted into irresponsibility, and individual rights have been corrupted by an interpretation of those rights in terms of the absence of rights for the other person.

Not only in this negative sense, however, but in the positive as well, we have witnessed an all but obsessive examination of one's self. Often this has been pursued to the extent that the impression is left that if one can but understand himself, everything else will automatically fall into place. Far be it from me to disparage self-understanding. It is important. Yet, is not an excessive preoccupation with one's self a strong indication that priority is perhaps being taken from the Lord and given to self?

Perverted individualism manifests itself in many ways in contemporary society. Rebellion on the college campuses, and among extremist groups generally, centers in an exalted concept of selfhood. The business or professional person who becomes so absorbed with individual success that he has little time for family and home, much less for God, also reflects a perverted individualism. Premarital and extramarital sexual relations often arise from the concept that only the individual and the fulfilment of his own physical desires are of fundamental importance. The thief, murderer, liar, or rapist in the jungle of our modern cities insists that only his own will is of significance. Often such an attitude penetrates the home, and one member or another of the family lives as though only his or her desires and interests should be of concern to the family group.

Second, *nationalism* may well obscure the necessity of giving priority to the Lord. No matter how devotedly one may love his country, such loyalty should never reach the point of removing national policy from the context of God's will. There is a place for patriotism within the will of God. Yet, it is not a shallow patriotism, false to divine revelation and blind to national ills. Rather, it is a patriotism which can face courageously the weaknesses of its national structure in the sure conviction that within the will of God there are counsel and truth adequate to point the way to the better life for all the nations of the world.

It is not easy to distinguish between nationalism and patriotism. Perhaps they may be distinguished, however, in one's attitude toward the oft quoted proverb, "My country, right or wrong." This is the battle cry of nationalism. For nationalism insists that devotion to country takes priority over all else, *right or wrong!*

True patriotism could never make such an assertion. Patriotism that is true to the sovereignty of God will say, "My nation!" and say it with a note of pride and enthusiasm. But true patriotism can never say, "My country, *right or wrong.*" My country must be right! This is in keeping with the teachings of prophetic religion, especially among Isaiah and Jeremiah. As Philip Hyatt has suggested,

> A nation must be courageous enough to criticize its own actions and policies, and not exhaust its energy simply in hating the enemy. . . . Prophetic religion . . . teaches that patriotism which looks only to immediate national advantage is shortsighted and false. A wide view of mankind based upon a profound understanding of the sphere of God's sovereignty will inform all true love of country.[6]

Third, *institutionalism* in religious life may well usurp the absolute loyalty that belongs to God. I recall a fine Christian lady, and a devoted Baptist, who once said to me, half-jokingly, "Sometimes I feel that I am more Baptist than I am Christian." Her very humor in making the remark denied her genuine conviction in this regard. Yet, do we not often approximate this view? Do we not reduce the total revelation of God concerning the church to our particular view of the church? There is a legitimate place for denominational loyalty. Yet are we the sole heirs to the kingdom of God?

Institutional forms of religion have unfortunately received more than their share of criticism in recent years. There must be some organization, some structure, to give expression to the faith that is ours. Certainly, few would ignore this simple yet basic principle. We need organizational structure in the local church, as well as in areas outside the community. There would be an appalling vacuum in Christendom without the hospitals, colleges, homes for children and aged people, mission agencies, Bible societies, and many other institutions which make possible the practical application of the faith which we treasure.

Yet, when these institutions claim such loyalty as to usurp the priority that belongs to God alone, an "institutionalism" emerges which is detrimental to the purposes of God. Seldom, if ever, does anyone intend for the organization to get so out of hand that it becomes an end in itself rather than a means of accomplishing the purposes of God. But this has happened. Note the Roman Catholic Church of the Middle Ages!

Fourth, *materialism* as a basic attitude toward life often robs God of the absolute loyalty that belongs to him. Philosophically, materialism insists that matter is the only reality and that everything in the world, including thought, will, and feeling, can be explained only in terms of matter. Obviously, such an interpretation of life leaves no room for the spiritual reality made relevant in the redemptive activity of God.

Many individuals who could not begin to define the philosophical implications of materialism are practicing materialists. A materialistic way of life insists that comfort, pleasure, and wealth are the highest goals in life.

Perhaps the most effective way of determining the degree to which you and I have become materialistically centered is to evaluate those objectives to which we give the greatest thought, time, attention, or priority in life. For example, what are your primary goals? Often we find that the goals established in the average home concern the purchase of new furniture, trading automobiles, whole-house air-conditioning, a longer than usual vacation, or some other material objective. Seldom are we as diligent in setting for ourselves spiritual and moral objectives.

There is nothing intrinsically wrong with seeking material goods in this life. One would be hard pressed to find biblical justification for the condemnation of acquiring new furniture, buying a second car, or some other material addition to one's possessions. Jesus never did blindly condemn material possessions. In fact, he insisted that God knows our need for certain material considerations. He was concerned with priority; seeking the kingdom of God *first,* then allowing all other things to fall into their proper focus (cf. Matt. 6:32–33).

Finally, *secularism* is a threat to absolute loyalty to God in our generation. In many ways secularism so closely parallels materialism as to appear almost identical. The word has many connotations. Among them is the understanding that secularism rejects any form of religious faith and worship. It is, therefore, more aggressive in its denial of the religious interpretation of life than is materialism. The two, materialism and secularism, are twin enemies to a religious interpretation of life.

To an increasing degree, God has been ruled out of any truly significant role in the world in which we live. Science and technology can discover the remedy to any ills which we confront, skilled diplomacy can handle any national emergency, and the "Great Society" is going to take care of all our personal needs from birth through death! Or, at least, so we are told. Relax, our leaders insist, we can create our own kingdom of good will!

Perhaps this has been unduly critical, for any sincere effort to remedy the ills of society should be met with sympathy from within the kingdom of God. Yet, it remains true that a secular society does not contain within itself the power necessary either to initiate significant reforms or to sustain such reforms once they are initiated. The Congress can pass legislation concerning equality of opportunity, racial justice, or any other areas of human relationships. But until the hearts of men are infilled by the transforming love of God there will be no satisfactory reconciliation within the human family.

Priority in our time.—Years ago the phrase "Peace in our time" became quite popular. It never did become a reality. The central theme of the First Commandment centers in "priority in our time." Will it ever become a reality?

Priority in our time. Is this too much for us to hope? Have we not learned through the three thousand years that separate us from this ancient word from God that only as we give priority to him shall we enter into that good life that he desires for us? Have not personal experiences taught us, sometimes tragically, that we cannot abandon our priority of God without suffering the inevitable consequences of despair, disillusionment, and defeat in the course of life? How long will it take us to learn that God really meant that his people were to have no loyalties before him, that absolute priority in life can be given to him alone?

There is one word that sums up the first of God's "ten words." It is the word PRIORITY!

Notes

1. From *The New Testament in Modern English*, © J. B. Phillips, 1958. Used with permission of The Macmillan Company.

2. Sydney Myers, *The Ten Words* (London: Independent Press, 1956), p. 25.

3. J. H. Oldham, *Life Is Commitment* (London: SCM Press, 1953), p. 57.

4. Ludwig Köhler, *Old Testament Theology* (Philadelphia: The Westminster Press, 1957), p. 36.

5. George Ernest Wright, in *The Interpreter's Bible*, I (New York: Abingdon Press, 1952), 356.

6. Philip Hyatt, *Prophetic Religion* (Nashville: Abingdon Press, 1947), p. 176.

2
SOVEREIGNTY

Do you have any household idols in your home? Does your church make any use of images or idols? If your answer is no to each of these questions, then what possible relevance does the Second Commandment have for your life? Its meaning is apparently clear. "You shall not make yourself a graven image, or any likeness of anything that is in heaven above, or that is in the earth beneath, or that is in the water under the earth; you shall not bow down to them or serve them" (Ex. 20:4–5). Many people see no more in this commandment than prohibition against graven images. But such an interpretation does not exhaust its meaning.

In essence, the Second Commandment says, "You shall not make yourself any graven image" (cf. Ex. 20:4–6; Deut. 5:8–10).

To arrive at the deeper meaning of the commandment, we must first ask why this prohibition was necessary. Why did the biblical revelation condemn the making of graven images? What understanding of the nature and character of God gave rise to the command? What attitude prevailed toward images in the Old Testament era? What did the making of an image imply concerning one's understanding of the LORD? It is for these basic principles that we must search, not just for the literal meaning of the commandment in the early history of Israel.

Second, if we can find the principles that gave rise to the commandment, then we may apply these principles to our contemporary understanding of the nature and character of God. In this manner the Bible will continue to speak the eternal and abiding word of God. Principles never change. In many instances, applications do change from one generation to another. Thus, while we do not face the problem of graven images in our own time, it may well be that we do face other issues which are directly related to the spirit or principle of the Second Commandment.

Ancient Near Eastern Religious Images

Whether in Egyptian, Mesopotamian, or Canaanite backgrounds, the gods were represented through images. Baal, the Canaanite god, was portrayed as a warrior with a thunderbolt as a spear. Anat, the sister of Baal, was portrayed as a warrior-goddess, and Astarte, was represented regularly in Egyptian reliefs as a naked female, standing upon a lion. In Egypt, although the chief gods were conceived in human form, most of the deities were depicted with the chief physical characteristics of animals: Horus with the head of a falcon, Anubis with the head of a jackal, Hathor with the horns of a cow. Even the Canaanite gods and goddesses were associated at times with animal figures; Baal and El are associated with the bull (probably because of its procreative power), Astarte (the biblical Ashtaroth) with the lion.

There are varied opinions concerning ancient man and his understanding of idols. Many insist that he thought the god existed as a spiritual reality, separate from the idol. Others contend that the god was so identified with the idol that the two were inseparable; the idol was the god, the god was the idol. More likely, in most instances the idol personified the spirit or principle associated with the god, and the god was not identical with the idol.

One should distinguish between this and popular thought,

however, for in the mind of the average worshiper the concrete form tended to supplant the attributes the idol symbolized. It is this latter attitude toward idolatry which was condemned so severely by both Jeremiah and Isaiah (cf. Jer. 10:1 ff.; Isa. 44:9 ff.). Isaiah sarcastically described the action of the man who cut down a tree and, having built a fire from part of it, then carved an idol—his god—from the remainder: "The rest of it he makes into a god, his idol; and falls down to it and worships it; he prays to it and says, 'Deliver me, for thou art my god!'" (Isa. 44:17).

In this example the idol had obviously been completely identified with the god.

In the religions of the ancient East the gods were personified powers of heaven, or earth, or the abyss. The basic and elemental forces of the world were often deified until an entire pantheon of gods was eventually created. The reduction of these powers to the concrete form of an image gave to ancient man an awareness both of revelation or presence, as well as the power of the god which would not have been present without the idol. In addition, it is rather widely agreed that possession of the idol gave ability to control or manipulate, to a greater or lesser degree, the god himself. Thus, the making of images was designed to express more than an act of devotion or worship. It arose out of the desire to insure the blessing and protection of the deity who was represented in the wood, clay, or stone.

This parallels the common belief in the ancient Near East that one could make an image of his enemy, then by placing a curse upon, or in some other manner abusing the image, cause harm to the actual enemy. Nations could also curse nations in this manner. The curse was written out on a tablet and then the tablet broken, symbolizing the ill fate of the enemy nation cursed. Along these same lines, therefore, the reduction of the god to an image was thought to have given the worshiper control or power he could not otherwise possess.

Principles in the Prohibition of Idolatry for Israel

The Second Commandment prohibited (1) the representation of the LORD in an image or idol, and (2) the use of images of created beings as an aid to the worship of the LORD. For example, the bull became the symbol of Baalism; Israel was to make no such images in her worship, even if the LORD was not actually identified with the image. What principles and what understanding of the LORD gave rise to this prohibition?

The nature of the biblical revelation.—That the nature of the biblical revelation is the primary concern of the Second Commandment stands in contrast to the view of many that the primary contribution of the command concerns the spirituality of God. That the LORD is absolute spirit is, of course, undeniable. But that Israel so clearly perceived this, or that this commandment seeks to implement such a conviction, is quite debatable. Thus, while it is true that God, who is spirit, cannot be adequately represented by an idol, the commandment is not ultimately grounded in this emphasis.

Pagan worshipers knew full well that deity is invisible, that it cannot be captured in an idol. Higher forms of religion in the ancient Near East attained a cosmic understanding of the gods to the end that they were by no means limited to the form of an idol. The important point to note concerning the Second Commandment is that first and foremost the image bears a revelation.

The gods were by and large personifications of the powers of heaven, earth, or the abyss. Thus, they were related to the world through a wide variety of phenomena within the created order. For example, the name of the high god Anu, in Sumerian, meant heaven, and corresponded to the Greek sky-god Zeus. Enlil's Sumerian name meant wind- or storm-god. Ea, third of the greater Babylonian gods, was designated "lord of wisdom." To him were ascribed magical knowledge, the arts and crafts, writing, building, and agriculture. Sin was the moon-god, Shamash the sun-god, Hadad the storm-god, and Ishtar the storm-goddess. Tiamat was goddess of chaos. Apsu was the god of the underworld ocean.

While these examples have been drawn from Babylonian and Assyrian religion, the same pattern prevailed in Egyptian and Canaanite religion. The gods personified some aspect of the created order, including man and his arts and crafts.

Since the god was himself the personification of some aspect of the created order, the image as a bearer of revelation equated the god with some aspect of creation.

This view of God's relationship to the created order was never acceptable to Israel. Although nature may reveal the glory of God, the LORD always stands above the created order. The revelation of the LORD came to Israel through the word. Hence, the continuing point of contact with Israel is to center in the word of the LORD, not in the deification of one aspect of God manifest in the world of nature.

Thus, the Second Commandment dealt, in depth, with the hidden way in which the LORD's revelation came about in history. The immediate and literal effect of the command meant that no idol would ever appear in the worship life of Israel. Yet, the commandment has far more than this to say to Israel—both ancient and modern. The commandment, in its own way, insists that Israel must continually hear afresh the revelation of God. For revelation is not in the concrete form of an idol but in the living presence of the LORD. The LORD does not speak in the rigid, fixed personifications of nature but in the living word that comes from the LORD. His will is not conveyed in images of brass, stone, or wood but in a living word of relevance and challenge to every new generation. This is the essence of the commandment.

The absolute freedom of the LORD.—In ancient religion the divine presence in the cultic image was an object of power at man's disposal. The reduction of the god to the concrete form of an idol made it possible for the worshiper to control, to a greater or lesser degree, the deity. This does not mean that every worshiper was seeking to manipulate the deity. But it does mean that, back of idolatry, this concept of control was basic.

Obviously, such a concept was totally incompatible with the true nature of the Lord. He was absolutely free and sovereign. Nothing existed which could encroach upon his freedom. Yet, to have made an idol of the Lord would have implied control of him by the worshiper. This is the inevitable course of idolatry: the manipulatory control of the deity by the worshiper. Negatively, the Second Commandment prohibits the control of the Lord by any person or power. Positively, it asserts the absolute freedom and sovereignty of the Lord.

Modern Expressions of Idolatry

The two principles discussed above are of continuing relevance for the life of every person within the covenant community. Stressing the method of revelation, and insisting upon the complete sovereignty of God, the commandment often runs at cross-purposes with much modern thought and action.

When are we guilty of violating the principles of the second of God's "ten words"?

First, we are guilty of modern idolatry when we limit the revelation of God to an absolutely rigid form, rather than receiving the revelation of God through the living word; a word that, though changeless, is ever changing to meet the shifting conditions of every generation. Idolatry, as we have seen, fixed revelation in the rigid form of stone or brass, personifying in the idol the phenomena of the ancient world. This was a perversion of godhood, according to the biblical revelation.

The Lord comes to us, not through concrete, never-changing laws, but through the living word which derives from his own will. Often this stands in marked contrast to our desires. Most of us want a fixed revelation of the will of God, applicable to every situation, demanding no searching of heart or trying of motivation on our own parts. We expect the biblical record, for example, to serve as a great code of law, embracing every facet of man's actions.

Yet, this is not the nature of the biblical revelation. There are issues which Israel faced that are no longer applicable to us. Contemporary crises exist about which the ancient person had never heard. So long as we take a rigid, literalistic view of the biblical record we will find no laws to cover many of our situations. But once we let God speak to us as living word, utilizing the Scriptures—especially his Son, there are no modern situations which the living Spirit of the biblical revelation will not cover.

Despite our desires, the revelation of God is not always as mechanical and rigid as we imagine, specifically in its implications. Many of us forget the words of our LORD who said that his understanding of the kingdom in its relation to man and his involvements was quite radical when compared with that which men had once understood. He was not guilty of an idolatry which fixes the revelation of God with rigidity. In this regard he reminded men that the combination of his new understanding of the word from God in its relationship to former understandings could best be compared with putting new wine in old wineskins, or sewing a new patch on an old garment (cf. Matt. 9:17). There was a radical discontinuity between the fresh inbreak of God through the living word and previous understandings of the nature and will of God.

We today fear a word from God, a gospel that is like new wine, fermenting and expanding, discontent, and unable to remain in old forms. We want a word from God that is stabilized so that we can handle it and control it. But when the word of God ceases to be living, active, fermenting in the heat of its own movement, and at times bursting old wineskins or tearing new patches off old garments, it will no longer be God's word but man's word that we confront. You cannot control a living word as a brass image!

Thus, when we become rigid in thought, unbending in will, unwilling to make adaptations in our understanding of the will of God and contemporary issues, we are likely to be guilty of modern idolatry. We will have then created our idols, which stand in marked contrast to the word of the living LORD.

Second, we are guilty of modern idolatry when we substitute one aspect of God's revelation for God himself. Ancient man saw God's creative wonder, but rather than worshiping God the Creator he personified some force of nature and worshiped it.

Whenever modern man substitutes or identifies an *expression* of God with the *essence* of God, he is again guilty of idolatry. Often, we substitute a witness to God for the essence of the LORD. The church is not God. The Bible is not God. The servants of God through the ministry of the church are not God. God always stands above and beyond church, Bible, or ministry. His Word breaks through their words on many occasions, but all must stand beneath his judgment. In the same manner, deeds of charity and social compassion, while legitimate witnesses to God and the godly life, should not supplant God but become the living evidence of his presence in our lives.

Third, when we limit God to our own understanding we are again guilty of idolatry. In ancient times a craftsman made an idol from his gold or silver, wood or stone. What pattern served to guide in the shaping of the idol? He made the idol according to his own understanding of the god. In like manner, too often today we continue to create God according to our own understanding.

Yet, God is greater than our greatest thought; higher than our highest idea or point of understanding. How often the average person limits God to his own understanding of the LORD! In the face of this, any difference of opinion is treated as the most violent of heresies. To limit God to my own understanding of him is the essence of pride. So long as God is God, he will stand beyond my highest understanding. Therefore, our own judgments and evaluations of the nature of God should be open. Then we will be susceptible to alteration and change in the face of new and unmistakable insight into the nature of God. Anything less than this is a modern form of idolatry.

Fourth, we are guilty of idolatry when we seek to control God, making him the means to achieving our own purposes rather than casting ourselves into the full expression of his will for us. In this regard we should remember the words of G. A. Smith:

> History is strewn with the errors of those who have sought from God something else than Himself. . . . Such are like the person who saw nothing in Christ but the recoverer of a bad debt, "Master, speak unto my brother that he divide the inheritance with me." . . . And though in these days we seek from the Bible many desirable things . . . yet all these will avail us little, until we have found behind them the living Character, the Will, the Grace, the Urgency, the Almighty Power, by trust in whom and communion with whom alone they are added unto us.[1]

The idol of ancient man was, in one sense, a means of controlling the deity. May we take care lest we become more concerned with controlling the LORD than with being controlled by him.

Fifth, we are guilty of modern idolatry when we "objectify" God, even in our thought, conceiving of his likeness to anything in heaven above or earth beneath. God is not to be equated with any objective, concrete form. He is not an object among other objects. He is not a person among other persons; differing essentially only in that he is more powerful, wise, or beneficent. He is not "the man upstairs." Nor is he the bearded patriarch sitting upon his throne. God lies beyond any attempt which we may make to express the essence of his being. Our ways of thinking of God often make him a part of the world. He is not part of the world. He is Creator, Redeemer, sustainer—one who stands completely beyond the range of his creation.

It is true that if we are to speak of God at all, we must do so in objective, human terms. Let us recognize that to use figures of speech does not capture the essence of God. Anything we say about God is open to the possibility of being a misrepresentation. We call him, and rightly so, Father, Shepherd, Light, salvation, rock, shield, defender, and a host of other expressive words. Yet, these are but feeble efforts to grasp something of his true nature. We can never say God *is* this or that. We can only say God is *like* this or that.

We insist upon objectifying God—equating him with our frail, human pictures that we sometimes childishly conceive. Because of this there are many in our generation who reject such an understanding of God. What modern atheism often revolts against is man's childish concept of God, which often is but an idol or an incorrect understanding, objectified and set forth as the true God. Consequently, what men often deny is a particular concept of God. And it may well be that the idea of God which they reject is a false idea that should be rejected.

Because we cannot limit God to human patterns of thought, our only language with God is the language of prayer and praise. The language of definition and complete comprehension evades us. In the confusion produced by our tower of Babel (cf. Gen. 11:1 ff.), we have lost the one tongue with which we could speak absolutely about the LORD. We can only wait with patient expectation for that time when we shall "know as we are known." Then perhaps we can describe him as he really is, without limitation. Until that time, however, our only language for God is the language of prayer. Anything else is modern idolatry.

Sovereign Lord

The second of God's "ten words" may be summed up in one word—SOVEREIGNTY.

Our LORD is alive, a living God who stands above the created order. He is not an idol, grinning like some Buddha nailed to the shelf lest he topple over. With freeness of movement, through his Spirit he comes to all who are open to him. To those who seek his will he yet speaks his living word of revelation. Through the Scriptures and through corporate and private worship, he continues to break through the shell of our misunderstanding into the core of our persons.

To deny the sovereign freedom of our LORD by imposing human limitations upon his revelation is to succumb to the continuing threat of modern idolatry.

Notes

1. Sydney Myers, *The Ten Words* (London: Independent Press, 1956), p. 34.

3
SINCERITY

The popular understanding of the Third Commandment concerns profanity. Obviously, profanity does "take the Lord's name in vain, or emptily." It robs or empties his name of the shining worth and significance that it ought to have. A high view of religious commitment will not breed a low view toward the name of the Lord. The name of God cannot be taken into the pits of filth and disrepute and retain the same sense of wonder and charm that it ought to exercise over our lives. No man can damn the name of God, reduce Jesus Christ to the level of four-letter vulgarities, and expect his religious life to be unmarred. As a matter of fact, the most serious effect of profanity is not upon God at all. He remains unmoved and untouched by the trifling misuse of his name. The individual who trifles with the name of God is the one who eventually must bear the ill effects which his thoughtless words have conceived. In smudging the name of the Lord, man leaves an indelible streak upon his own life, as well as his communion with the Lord.

While profane use of the name of God is included within the broad scope of the Third Commandment, its true significance is much deeper.

Understanding the Commandment

"You shall not take the name of the Lord your God in vain" (Ex. 20:7; Deut. 5:11).

Two elements which are of absolute importance for understanding the commandment are the meaning of the "name" in ancient Israel and the connotation of the word "vanity." Literally translated, the essence of the command is: "You shall not lift up the name of the Lord (Yahweh) your God for nothingness—emptiness, vacuity."

The *name* had significance in Israel, and the ancient Near East generally, which it does not have for modern man. Today, a name is no more than a means of distinguishing between one person and another. In Israel, however, one's name meant something. It summed up the essence of the person. So much was this the case that in one sense the name was the person. Today, for example, a nickname often derives from an outstanding characteristic of the individual—"shorty" or "red" in some circles; "egghead" among yet other circles portrays the essence of the individual.

The experiences of Jacob illustrate the implications of the name in Israel. After Jacob had obtained Isaac's blessing, Esau responded, "Is he not rightly named Jacob? For he has supplanted me these two times" (Gen. 27:36). The name Jacob meant "he takes by the heel" or "he supplants." His name summed up the essence of his personality; Jacob was a supplanter! Later, at the ford of the Jabbok River, Jacob had an unusual experience with the Lord (cf. Gen. 32:22 ff.). It affected all of his life. He was never the same person after that encounter. Because the *man* Jacob was changed, his *name* was changed to "Israel," meaning he who strives with God. Thus, the name expressed what Jacob now was.

The names of the prophets also reflect the manner in which the name summed up the essence of the person. "Isaiah" means salvation (is) of the Lord. "Jeremiah" means the Lord hurls; "Malachi," my messenger.

The name given to Jesus also reflects this ancient understanding; You shall "call his name Jesus: for he shall save his people from their sins" (Matt. 1:21). His name summed up our Lord's central purpose: "The Son of man is come to seek and to save" (Luke 19:10).

Despite the similarity of the ancient practice with the modern nickname, however, it involved far more than the modern practice. In ancient times the person was felt actually to have been present in the name; present in a manner in which he would not have been present apart from the name. Because of this, often there was some hesitation in the giving of one's name. The angel of the Lord said to Manoah, "Why do you ask my name, seeing it is wonderful?" (Judg. 13:18). To know the name in the ancient Near East also gave power over the person whose name was known. To name a person implied authority or control over the person. This is quite likely why Adam is portrayed as naming the animals. Such action demonstrated his role as sovereign (cf. Gen. 1:26 f.; 2:19 f.). In the closing days of the monarchy, the king of Babylon changed the name of Mattaniah to Zedekiah, obviously as a demonstration of the authority of the Babylonian power (cf. 2 Kings 24:17).

As a consequence of all these factors, the "name" came to play an important part in the theology of Israel. For example, in calling Israel out of Egypt God revealed his name—the Lord (cf. Ex. 3:13 ff.). In revealing his "name" the Lord had revealed himself. At the very heart of Israelite worship was the phrase "call on the name of the Lord" (cf. Gen. 12:8; 13:4; 21:33; 1 Kings 18:24).

The Lord may dwell in the heavens, but he chooses a place on earth where he can "make his name dwell" (Deut. 12:5; 14:24). His name lives at the place of worship (cf. Deut. 26:15). Because of this, the Lord saves by his name (cf. Psalm 43:1). Men find protection in his "name" (Psalm 20:1), and his name is a tower of refuge (cf. Prov. 18:10).

The name of the Lord was revelatory to the point that in the very name there was the *presence* of the Lord. Consequently, his name had to be protected from usage that would detract from the praise and respect due him. Stated positively, this meant that Israel had to hallow the name of the LORD, even as Jesus was later to teach men to pray, "Hallowed be thy name" (Matt. 6:9).

Eventually men would not even pronounce the name "Yahweh," lest they profane it. When Yahweh appeared in a passage, the reader pronounced "Lord." This is the reason why "LORD" appears with all capitals as opposed to Lord in the same English translations.

Why did this commandment appear in the midst of those commandments concerned with the essential nature of the LORD's character and demand? Simply because there is an essential point of connection between it and the Second Commandment. Other nations had their idols, Israel had the LORD's name. Just as the Second Commandment insisted that God was revealed through the Word and not through idols, the Third Commandment insists that the name as a primary medium of revelation must be protected against anything that would violate the sacred nature of God's self-disclosure. Men are, therefore, to be exceedingly careful with the name of the LORD because (1) the LORD is present in his name and (2) the name (as spoken word) is the essence of the biblical revelation. The name played the same role for Israel that the idol played in non-Israelite religions.

Why are we to protect the name of the LORD from profane use and abuse? When we have the name, we have the essence of the person. God reveals himself not in graven images but in his name. Thus, to violate the name is to violate the LORD.

What did the Old Testament mean when it insisted that men were not to "take the LORD's name in vain?" What implications did the word have to the Old Testament reader or listener?

The word "vain" or "vanity" (*shaw'*) has the literal meaning of emptiness—a vacuum, nothingness, hollow, unfilled, vacant. It is used in fifty-two Old Testament verses. In twenty-three verses it means nothingness, instability, or purposelessness. For example, unless "the LORD build the house, they labour in vain" (Psalm 127:1). Idols are spoken of as vain, i.e., nothingness (cf. Psalm 31:7; Jonah 2:9; Jer. 18:15). Offerings are also at times described as vain, in the sense that they are empty of true meaning or significance (cf. Isa. 1:13). Men who are dedicated to no purpose are said to be "determined to go after vanity" (Hos. 5:11, RSV). With unrepentant Israel, God's judgment has been futile, "in vain" (cf. Jer. 2:30). Some men say, "It is vain to serve God" (Mal. 3:14).

The second category of usage concerns those passages, twenty-four, which have to do with emptiness of speech. In such cases the word *shaw"* is often translated falsehood (cf. Prov. 30:8; Hos. 12:2; Job 31:5) or "lies" (cf. Isa. 59:4; Ezek. 13:8). It may also be translated "false" (Ezek. 12:24; Ex. 23:1). The basic meaning is clear, however, for whatever is false, a falsehood, or a lie is empty of truth; it has no inner reality. It is a vacuum.

The third category of usage concerns worthless men. Individuals whose lives are empty of meaning and purpose are often characterized by *shaw"*. There are five verses that use the word in this manner. The psalmist said that he did not "sit with false men" or, better, worthless men (26:4). Job said, "He [God] knows worthless men" (11:11). Isaiah had in mind worthless motives (cf. 5:18).

A detailed examination of the Old Testament verses which use the word *shaw"* (vain) indicates that the basic meaning is always retained. The word always conveys the idea of nothingness, emptiness, vacuity, or purposelessness.

Biblical Implications of the Command

The Third Commandment prohibits the taking up of the LORD's name for a worthless purpose. One is not to take lightly the name of the LORD. His name is not to be treated in such fashion as either to suppose that it is insignificant in content or to lead others to conclude that the LORD's name is meaningless. Because the name is the essence of revelation, the member of the covenant community is to look upon the name with absolute reverence and seriousness. What the *idol* is to the noncovenantal person, the *name* is to the covenant member. Consequently, the name is to be used only in a cultic or worship setting. If it is used outside the worship setting, it is to be treated with the highest respect.

Can one be any more specific in the application of this commandment to life in ancient Israel? Many competent scholars have concluded that the commandment is a warning against using the name of the LORD to attest to something that is false. Thus, false swearing is felt to be at the center of the commandment. An amplification of this is found in Leviticus 19:12: "You shall not swear by my name falsely, and so profane the name of your God: I am the LORD." It seems clear that false swearing would violate the commandment. To swear by the LORD's name was quite acceptable in ancient Israel. His name was used to attest to the truth of the statement made. "You shall fear the LORD . . . and swear by his name (Deut. 6:13; cf. Deut. 10:20; Lev. 19:12). Only false swearing is prohibited. The Old Testament specifically relates the commandment to false swearing.

Despite this, however, it seems that false swearing is too limited a view of the meaning of the commandment. The word *shaw"* meant more than falsehood. It is my own conviction that it carried evil connotations which went far beyond the limited concept of falsehood. Gerhard von Rad has suggested that the word may have had magical connotations. He cites S. Mowinckel to the effect that "even in Israel people were at times liable to use Jahweh's name for sinister purposes dangerous to the community."[1]

Failure to hallow the revelation that had come to Israel and to abandon the worship of the LORD was to profane the name. "You shall not give any of your children to devote them by fire to

Molech, and so profane the name of your God: I am the Lord" (Lev. 18:21). Again, "He has given one of his children to Molech, defiling my sanctuary and profaning my holy name" (Lev. 20:3). Disloyalty to one's faith could, therefore, profane the name of the Lord. Is it not likely that such action should also be considered within the scope of the Third Commandment?

Thus, any action that denied the centrality of the Lord's revelation through the word, his name, was to take his name "in vain."

Contemporary Relevance of the Commandment

Understanding of the contemporary relevance of the commandment is grounded in at least two presuppositions. First, in biblical thought one's attitude toward the name was synonymous with one's attitude toward the revelation of God. Because the revelation of God came in the living word as opposed to idols, it was imperative that the name of the Lord be given the hallowed position which the uniqueness of his revelation demanded. Second, the commandment was addressed to members of the covenant community; those whom the Lord had redeemed. Consequently, any legitimate interpretation of the commandment must address itself to those who stand within the covenant. The commandment is concerned, therefore, with the attitude which those within the covenant take toward the supreme revelation of God.

To take the Lord's name in vain involves far more than profanity or perjury under oath; even one's swearing falsely by the name of the Lord. Rather, to take the Lord's name in vain is to take a lighthearted, flippant attitude toward the revelation of God which empties or robs it of its absolute significance. In essence, the commandment deals with the sincerity of religious commitment; the degree of faithfulness which men within the covenant have toward the divine revelation. To take up the Lord's name—perhaps upon one's self—in a meaningless way is to violate the commandment. Within this commandment one stands face to face with the seriousness of the biblical revelation. Are there evidences that we take an "empty" attitude toward the divine revelation? Consider the following.

First, *our manner of speech* may reflect a violation of the commandment. Not only in profanity but also in other ways in which we speak of God, we may "take his name in vain."

If you would apply a revealing test, ask not whether your words take the LORD's name in vain, but whether your words honor the LORD. Of course, many times words are simply habitual and a part of our culture. They do not necessarily reflect one's true religious commitment. Not every person who so uses the name of God really wants to "damn God." But language *is* symptomatic, pointing out inclinations toward superficiality in religious commitment.

Second, *our way of life* may reflect that we are guilty of taking the LORD's name "in vain." When men identify with the church as a part of one's social heritage as opposed to a union with the living Christ, identification with him has been "in vain." In such cases we as Christians have literally taken his name, the name of Christ, upon ourselves; and we have taken it for "emptiness" or "nothingness" when we do not allow him to transform our lives. To claim that we have entered into the quality of life outlined within the biblical revelation, to take the LORD's name upon ourselves, and at the same time relegate that way of life to the irrelevant and the insignificant is to violate the commandment. We take the LORD's name in vain when faith is manipulated as though it were a bargain basement prize, and God is exploited to our own advantage.

Third, *our commitment* often reflects a violation of the Third Commandment. Any commitment less than the absolutely serious is a violation of this word from God. Attitudes of indifference and unconcern toward our commitment betray that we have "taken the LORD's name in vain."

The Third Commandment may be summarized in this one word—SINCERITY. God demands that we enter into covenant with him in an absolutely sincere commitment.

Notes

1. Gerhard von Rad, *Old Testament Theology*, I (London: Oliver & Boyd, 1962), p. 183.

4
SANCTITY

For many believers the sabbath, or Lord's Day, has remained a holy day. But there are multitudes for whom the Lord's Day is a day of grass-cutting, lounging, and amusement. Is this wrong? Should we expect those outside the community of faith to subscribe to the same interpretation of the day that we follow? Can we draw up a list of definitive actions which may be taken on six days but must be omitted on the seventh? In essence, how are we to understand and relate the implications of the Fourth Commandment, which says, "Remember the sabbath day to keep it holy," to the complexities of modern life?

Forms of the Commandment

The Fourth Commandment is the first of the Ten Commandments to reveal any significant variation as one compares its statement in Exodus 20 with the parallel form in Deuteronomy 5. There are six points of difference between the two statements.

First, Exodus uses "remember," while Deuteronomy uses "observe" (guard or keep) the sabbath day. Both words convey the same idea, "to keep it holy." This could literally be translated, "for the purpose of keeping it holy." The words are infinitives, not imperatives, assuming that the day will be remembered or observed, and that such observance is "for the purpose of making holy [for the purpose of setting apart] the sabbath day." Thus, both statements are in exact agreement concerning the primary purpose of God in this area.

Second, Deuteronomy adds to the opening phrase the words, "as the LORD your God commanded you." The command is not found in the conclusion of the phrase in Exodus.

Third, Exodus includes among the domestic animals only "your cattle." Deuteronomy has the elongated phrase "your ox, or your ass, or any of your cattle."

Fourth, Deuteronomy adds "that your manservant and your maidservant may rest as well as you." This does not appear in the Exodus statement.

Fifth, Exodus mentions the creative activity of God and grounds the observance of the sabbath in the fact that "in six days the LORD made heaven and earth, the sea, and all that is in them, and rested the seventh day." Deuteronomy does not mention creation and God's rest at all but makes reference to the Exodus experience. "You shall remember that you were a servant in the land of Egypt, and the LORD your God brought you out thence with a mighty hand and an outstretched arm; *therefore* the LORD your God commanded you to keep the sabbath day."

Sixth, Exodus makes no appeal in the conclusion of the commandment. The writer rests his case in the statement: "Therefore the LORD blessed the sabbath day and hallowed it." Deuteronomy, however, makes no reference to the blessing and hallowing of the day: "Therefore the LORD your God commanded you to keep the sabbath day."

Originally the Commandments were briefer statements. The lengthier comments were added by men, inspired of God, living after the time of Moses.

Intent of the Commandment

From the above comparison of the two forms of the commandment, what appears to have been the intention of the commandment for the faith of Israel?

First, the central purpose of the commandment lay in the sanctity of the seventh day. It was to be a holy day, set apart for the Lord.

"Holiness" meant complete dedication to the Lord. It might involve separation from the world in the process. But the main thrust of the concept was positive, not negative. Therefore, the biblical view of holiness involved the idea of dedication to the Lord, not separation from the world. Often this distinction is not clearly emphasized. As a result, far too many today have a negative view of holiness. This was reflected in the story carried several years ago in a national magazine. The account concerned an advertisement to the effect that a hyperconservative school was located "fifteen miles from any known source of sin." Most of us have not been able to get that far away!

Another concept of holiness is that objects were holy because of their relationship to the Lord, not in and of themselves. Jerusalem was a "holy" city. The Temple was holy, as were the utensils used in sacrifice. There were sacred sites and objects throughout the land of Israel. Sacred, however, not of themselves or their "goodness," but because they were related to the Lord. It is extremely important to note that "holiness" indicates a quality of relationship with the Lord more than a quality which inheres in a person or object. *Holiness is a relationship.*

In its present form the Bible presents two statements of the Fourth Commandment. While there are significant differences, they should be viewed as complementary rather than contradictory. Indeed, the two forms reflect what was pointed out earlier: The revelation of God does not come to man with rigidity of form like that of idols but in the living word of God. Every generation must struggle, under the leadership of God's spirit, to find within the Bible the living, growing revelation of the complete will of God.

Consequently, the two forms of the commandment simply reflect the unfolding of the divine revelation of God concerning the observance of a holy day by people within the framework of the covenant. Back of both forms of the commandment there was probably a briefer statement of the command (much like the brevity of the later commandments). The explanatory and hortative statements were probably the work of later men, inspired by the Lord. They are minor details that are relatively unimportant; e.g., Exodus mentions only "beast" while Deuteronomy mentions "ox, ass, or cattle." Literal dictation of the various parts of the Bible is not prerequisite to expression of the will of God. God is well able to communicate his will through slightly different expressions.

The sanctity of life and time.—Ancient men lived in a world of holiness in the positive sense and of taboo in the negative sense. Life and the world alike were filled with the presence of God. Consequently, the world was also filled with the mysterious holiness of God. An overpowering sense of awe and dread, mingled with fear, filled the entire created order.

This was no less true in Israel than in the ancient Near East generally. The nation was holy, as were tribes, men, and places. Because men, property, space, and time were all consecrated to the LORD, the world, as well as all of man's involvements, was proclaimed as belonging to the LORD. There was no division of life into the sacred and the secular; all things were his! Because they were his, they shared his holiness. Holiness had a way, therefore, of proclaiming that the holy object belongs to the LORD.

Out of this background the idea of a holy day may be better understood. It is quite likely that in setting one day apart as holy to the LORD, the writer was in a sense claiming all of life as the holy sphere of God's domain. The whole was symbolically summed up in the part. This principle appears, for example, in offering the firstfruits to the LORD. The entire harvest was summed up in the offering of the firstfruits.

There is a sense, therefore, in which the sabbath, by setting aside one day in seven as a day uniquely holy to the LORD, thus proclaimed the sanctity of all life. As George Jackson has suggested, "Just as a landowner, over whose property the public are [sic] allowed to make a way, will sometimes close it during one day in the year that thereby he may show that the land is his every day, so God decreed that one day should be set apart for Him, that men might learn that to Him not one but all our days belong."[1]

Sabbath Observance in Israel

What were the primary characteristics of sabbath observance in Israel?

First, the day was one of rest. The Commandments themselves make no mention of formal worship. The day belonged to God, not to man for the pursuit of his own interests. By this, man was reminded that his days were not his own. They belonged to the LORD (cf. Ex. 31:14–16; Lev. 16:31; 23:3, 32; 25:4).

Second, the sabbath became a day of worship in the religious life of Israel. Leviticus, for example, refers to it not only as a day of rest but as "a holy convocation" (Lev. 23:3). Ezekiel also referred to the sabbath in this manner. "The people of the land shall worship at the entrance of that gate before the LORD on the sabbaths and on the new moons" (Ezek. 46:3). "New moon" was seemingly a monthly religious celebration in Israel, and the reference of sabbath and new moon in the same context also underscores the relationship between worship and the sabbath (cf. Amos 8:5; 2 Kings 4:23; Isa. 1:13).

Strangely enough, the Old Testament makes no effort to specify all that characterizes "rest" on the sabbath. However, sabbath observance prohibited business activities. "If the peoples of the land bring in wares or any grain on the sabbath day to sell, we will not buy from them on the sabbath or on a holy day" (Neh. 10:31). The day gave priority to the LORD: "If you turn back your foot from the sabbath, from doing your pleasure on my holy day, and call the sabbath a delight and the holy day of the Lord honorable; if you honor it, not going your own ways, or seeking your own pleasure, or talking idly; then you shall take delight in the Lord" (Isa. 58:13–14).

As is so often the case of structured religious form, the time came when Israel actually abused the commandment in her attempt to keep it. By building a hedge of minute laws about the sabbath, Jewish leaders sought to preserve its meaning. Actually, however, the very attempt to force the revelation of God into a rigid form of mechanical law destroyed the vitality of the commandment. The revelation of God must come to us in living word, addressing itself to the changing circumstances of man's involvements.

In the times immediately preceding and during the life of Jesus an all but innumerable mass of sabbath laws emerged to regulate the observance of the day. The tragedy of these laws could well serve as a warning to those today who would legislate sabbath observance, even among those who make no religious commitment, Christian or Jewish. You cannot legislate holiness. It emerges from a relationship with the Lord.

Jewish law specified thirty-nine types of work that could not be pursued on the sabbath. Within each of these there were numerous subdivisions. Ornaments could not be worn, lest the individual take them off to show them to another and thereby "bear a burden" on the sabbath. A radish could be dipped in salt, but could not be left, since this would make a pickle—work on the sabbath! To cut a mushroom was a double sin; work was involved in cutting it, and the growth of the new mushroom. No food could be cooked on the sabbath. The coals had to be removed from the oven preceding the sabbath, lest one confront the temptation to cook on the sabbath. Edersheim concludes that Jewish law "in its anxiety to ensure its [the sabbath's] most exact observance, changed the spiritual import of its rest into a complicated code of external and burdensome ordinances." [2]

Jesus' Interpretation of the Sabbath

In the face of a legalism which exalted the day above human personality, Jesus taught that the day was made for man; not the man for the day (Mark 2:27). Indeed, Jesus extended his authority over the day to the point that he claimed to be Lord of the sabbath; the day must stand beneath the person of Jesus Christ (cf. Matt. 12:8). Insisting that it was lawful to do good on the sabbath (Mark 3:4), Jesus healed (cf. Mark 3:1 ff.). He also permitted his disciples to pluck grain on the sabbath to satisfy their hunger (cf. Mark 2:23 ff.). In his evaluation of conduct appropriate to the sabbath, Jesus was influenced more by human need than by legal prescription. He always sublimated the mechanical understanding of the revelation of God to a living word that came from God in the face of the immediate situation.

Modern application of Jesus' principles would do much to clarify the role of the sabbath, or the Lord's Day, for the contemporary believer. Whatever our specific conclusions concerning what is or is not appropriate activity for the day, let us remember that the day was made for man, not man for the sabbath. Its humanitarian concern is as old as Deuteronomy (cf. 5:14 f.).

Jewish Sabbath and Christian Lord's Day

"Why do we worship on the first day of the week instead of the seventh like the Bible says?" I can still remember asking this question as a Junior boy. Also, I can still see the deacon, embarrassed for lack of an answer, who suddenly discovered he was needed in the records office. He never did answer my question. Mature reflection reveals that the question had an innocent twist at its conclusion that was not appropriate. Many today often raise the same question, however.

There is no specific command in the New Testament for the

Christian community to begin worship on the first day of the week. Actually, there is no command to the effect that the church was to observe any day of the week. The movement of the early church to worship on the first day of the week likely went through at least three steps.

First, for some period of time the early Jewish Christians worshiped on the Jewish sabbath, even as the temple and synagogue were used as places of worship in the beginning. For Gentile Christians sabbath observance was never enforced. They were exempt, particularly from Jewish institutions.

Second, while there was no specific command that the sabbath be observed, the need for a day of worship was no doubt felt quite early. There was the longing for worship, prayer, and fellowship that finds its fulfilment in corporate worship.

Third, since Judaism already contained the concept of a weekly day of rest, it was quite natural that this should also be embodied in the Christian community. What more logical day was there for the early church than the first day of the week—the day of their Lord's resurrection? Because of the adoption of the first day, therefore, there is a sense in which every Sunday is resurrection Sunday.

In c. A.D. 112, Pliny, the Roman, submitted a report to the Emperor Trajan concerning the Christians. The following excerpt makes reference to a "fixed day" on which they worshiped.

> On an appointed day they had been accustomed to meet before daybreak, and to recite a hymn antiphonally to Christ, as to a god, and to bind themselves by an oath, not for the commission of any crime, but to abstain from theft, robbery, adultery, and breach of faith, and not to deny a deposit when it was claimed.[3]

This "fixed day" which Pliny mentioned was probably the first day of the week. While there is no absolutely conclusive evidence, there are indications within the New Testament that the early church met consistently on the first day of the week.

Luke referred to the time: "On the first day of the week, when we were gathered together to break bread" (Acts 20:7). Also, Paul assumed a consistent gathering of the church on the first day of the week (cf. 1 Cor. 16:1 f.).

One's attitude toward the sabbath remained, however, a matter of conscience in the teaching of Paul (cf. Rom. 14:5 f.; Gal. 4:9 ff.). But as time passed, the emerging Christian church eventually adopted the first day of the week as its day of worship.

In conclusion, lest one become disturbed at the changed attitude of the New Testament church toward the Old Testament sabbath, it should be remembered that even the Old Testament portrayed a changing attitude toward the day. Exodus commended it because of the creative activity of God. By the time Deuteronomy was written, it was related to the redemptive activity of the LORD in the Exodus. The New Testament simply took the process one step further and altered the day, making the day of rest and worship fall on the first day as testimony to the resurrection of the Christ.

Your Life and the Sabbath

In the midst of the complexities of modern life, the sabbath, or Lord's Day, may be a serious problem for many individuals of deep faith. What should or should not be done on the sabbath? How is the contemporary Christian to respond to recreational activity on the Lord's Day? Are Sunday closing laws, or so-called Blue Laws, legitimate? While these questions can be answered only in the conscience of the believer before God, the following suggestions may be of help.

First, the sanctity of one day in seven, the Lord's Day for Christians, is essentially a covenant relationship. It is obligatory only upon those who have been redeemed and entered into covenant with the LORD. It is highly debatable whether Sunday closing laws are legitimate on a religious basis. By what reason should a noncovenant citizen be forced to observe a day sacred only to members of a covenant community? Sunday laws are legitimate essentially as they provide for the social betterment of the people. Such closings making it possible for families to be united in rest and recreation together, as well as offering consistent periods of rest to the worker. If legitimate, they are so because of grounds other than the religious.

Second, one's attitude toward the sabbath should be grounded in the positive aspects of holiness. Our conduct on this day should reflect our consecration to the LORD. If the Bible did not formulate specific forms of recreation and other activities that were acceptable or nonacceptable, should we, at this late date, attempt to legislate for anyone other than ourselves? Each person must decide for himself, under the leadership of God's Spirit, what conduct is appropriate for him on the Lord's Day. One should always be guided, however, by the realization that one's action on this day, especially, is to epitomize his relationship to the LORD.

Third, observance of the Lord's Day should serve as a constant reminder that every day is his day. The whole is consecrated by the part; the entire week is symbolically compressed into one day of the week. We err, therefore, when we believe that forms of conduct acceptable to God on Monday through Saturday are unacceptable on Sunday. Activity should be examined not solely on the basis of what day it may occur on but whether it is right as we understand the will of God.

Fourth, activity on Sunday should be governed by the witness one's life may be to others. Quite often, Christians refrain from certain activities on Sunday, not because they feel the activity to be improper for Sunday, but because of traditional views which prevail concerning the particular action. The stronger brother is under obligation to his weaker brother in this matter. Consequently, there may be many times in your life when a particular activity on Sunday would be perfectly legitimate. Yet, you may refrain from it lest by your example someone else be caused to stumble. Sabbath conduct may be a most effective means of a silent, Christian witness to the grace of God.

Fifth, the commandment is not stated in the imperative mood. The initial parts of both commandments agree in simply assuming that you will "remember" or "observe" the sabbath day to keep it holy. If observance of the Lord's Day must be grounded in command, whether by God or by the state, then it is highly questionable whether the observance will have any spiritual benefit to the individual. Rewarding observance of the commandment is grounded in an act of free will in which a person seeks to consecrate one day in seven as a symbol of the consecration of all of life and space.

The one word which captures the essence of the commandment is SANCTITY. The sanctity of one day out of seven symbolizes the sanctity of all life. Every day is a sabbath day because every day is sacred, for every day belongs to the Lord. The sanctity of the sabbath effectively proclaims the believer's understanding of the essential sanctity of all time and space.

Notes

1. George Jackson, *The Ten Commandments* (Edinburgh and London: Anderson & Ferrier, 1898), pp. 84–85.
2. Alfred Edersheim, *Jesus the Messiah*, II (Grand Rapids: Wm. B. Eerdmans Publishing Co., 1947), p. 787. Cf. pp. 777 ff.
3. Henry Bettenson (ed.), *Documents of the Christian Church* (New York and London: Oxford University Press, 1947), p. 6.

5
UNITY

As significant as the home may be in modern life, it was thought to have been even more significant in ancient Israel. So much was this the case that for many years not the individual but the nation, tribe, or family was considered as the primary unit in the covenant. While *the individual* was taken into consideration at all times, and individual responsibility was ultimately given its rightful place (cf. Jer. 31:29 ff.; Ezek. 18:1 ff.), *the group* was always of primary importance in Old Testament thought. In early Israel one was first an Israelite, a member of the covenant community; second, a member of a particular tribe or village; third, of the house of a particular elder; fourth, the immediate son of a particular man; and last of all, he was an individual.

Because of this, it was imperative that the home—which more often than not included all those directly related by blood, plus servants, rather than the modern husband, wife, and children—remain stable and harmonious. Psychologically and, to a degree, theologically, a man was felt to have been present in his son(s). It was for this reason that the birth of sons was so important; not only the name had to be preserved but the father lived on in the sons.

The Fifth Commandment says, "Honor your father and your mother" (cf. Ex. 20:12; Deut. 5:16).

The home continues to be a point of pivotal importance for

society. The breakdown of practically all civilizations has been preceded by the disintegration of the home. It is within the home that formative character traits are developed. One learns, or fails to learn, how to live harmoniously within society and to respond creatively to his environment. The noble example of a father and mother within the home is a positive factor which cannot be duplicated by the machinery of a thousand social agencies.

Would not the kingdom of God come as a transfusion into the lives of multitudes if the home would once again recapture its centrality as an agent of the kingdom of God?

In a much higher sense than originally intended, the words of the psalmist sound a positive recall to the centrality of the LORD for the vitality of the home in contemporary society. "Unless the LORD builds the house, those who build it labor in vain" (127:1). The purpose of the Fifth Commandment is twofold. First, it brings the home within the structure of the covenant's primary concern, making it first among those commandments that serve to relate man's action in the human sphere to the larger purposes of God. Second, it underscores the fact that the fulfilment of God's purposes for the home is grounded in the sense of unity that ties one generation to another—one member of the parent-child relationship to the other.

If man is united with God through being made in his image, is it surprising that God expects unity to manifest itself in the most basic area of human relationships, the home? In manifesting the image of God through human action, man begins by recognizing the unity that he shares within the family structure.

Understanding the Commandment

While the commandment is relatively clear in its implications, there are several areas that are often either ignored or not clarified.

First, the commandment should be understood against the background of its covenantal setting. It is a demand from the

LORD upon those who have entered into covenant with him, thus pledging themselves to manifest his nature and character in their life involvements. This has several implications.

For example, the covenantal background of the command reflects the way in which attitudes toward God are intended to govern attitudes in life. By bringing the family relationship into the context of the covenant, the LORD raises this relationship to foremost importance. What one believes about God is not a matter for the temple or sanctuary alone. It permeates the most personal relationships of life, even the attitude one has toward his parents.

Also, it is important that one recognize that the covenant was made with adult, male members of the community. The covenant was not made with children. Neither, was it made with women (for example, the rite of the covenant was circumcision). The ancient world was all but literally a "man's world." Of course, both children and women were included within the spirit and principle of the commandments. But they were included because they were members of the family to whom the covenant blessing and demand were mediated through the husband-father-owner relationship.

Therefore this commandment should not be lightly treated by the adult, as though it were the urgings of God toward a preschool child to "be nice to your mother and father." The commandment meant much more than this. It cut to the very core of man's relationship—on the adult level—with his own parents.

The literal meaning of the verb which we translate "honor" means to be heavy, weighty, burdensome, honored. It is not absolutely clear how the concept of "honor" emerged from the basic idea of weight or heaviness, but many believe that it was associated with the weight or burden of one's possessions. In biblical thought, possessions were related to honor in two ways. First, the person of great wealth, weight of possessions, was thought to have been uniquely blessed of God; hence, honored. This was, of course, a continuing problem for the theology of Israel. It was not until the book of Job that it was clearly illustrated that many times a man served God "for nothing." Second, the person with great possessions or weight was accorded a significant position in the ancient community; i.e., honored. We see something of this same idea when we hear the slang expression, "He carries a lot of weight in that community."

The word *kavedh*, translated "honor," has a colorful and significant history in the Old Testament. For example, it is used not only of one's parents (cf. Ex. 20:12; Deut. 5:16; Mal. 1:6) but of individuals who are to be honored (cf. 1 Sam. 2:29; 15:30; 2 Sam. 10:3).

Objects and institutions also received honor in Israel. The place of God's dwelling is characterized by honor (cf. Isa. 60:13), and men are called upon to honor the sabbath (cf. Isa. 58:13). Especially, however, is God himself described as the one to whom honor is given (cf. 1 Sam. 2:30*a*; Isa. 24:15; 25:3; 43:20; Psalms 22:24; 50:15,23; Prov. 14:31; Isa. 43:23; Isa. 29:13; Prov. 3:9).

Honor (*kavedh*) as a verb is the direct predecessor of the noun "glory" or "honor" (*kavodh*). Over and over in the Old Testament, the word "glory" is used to describe both the nature of God and the response that he strikes in the lives of his people. Eventually it became a synonym for the presence of the LORD himself. The "glory" of the LORD filled the temple (cf. 1 Kings 8:11); his "glory" is to be declared among the nations (cf. 1 Chron. 16:24); his "glory" is above the heavens (cf. Psalm 8:1). Indeed, Isaiah felt that the whole earth was full of the "glory" of the LORD (cf. Isa. 6:3). Ultimately it was understood as the "burning presence" of the Lord (cf. the way fire and light are associated with the "glory of the Lord").

When the Hebrew Bible was translated into Greek, the translators used an interesting word to capture the meaning of the Fifth Commandment. They did not use the word *doxa* (glory), so often used of the "glory of the Lord," but the verb *timaō*. In nonbiblical Greek (as well as that of the Septuagint) it is used of the honor rendered to superiors, as by men to gods, by men to their elders, rulers, or guests; even of the honor bestowed by gods upon a man. In the New Testament the word is used to fix the value or price of Christ. "They took the thirty pieces of silver, the *price* of him on whom a price had been set by some of the sons of Israel" (Matt. 27:9). In still other contexts of the New Testament the noun means "a valuing." "You were bought with a price (*timēs*)" (1 Cor. 6:20; cf. also Acts 4:34; 5:2; 1 Cor. 7:23). Hence, the translators of the Fifth Commandment used a word for honor which meant the value of a person or object. Thus, in keeping with this, one could paraphrase the commandment, "Thou shalt value, or treasure, your father and your mother."

Seriousness of the Command

With this background, we may understand more clearly the serious implications of the demand that we honor our parents. "Honor" implies the ascription of the greatest possible "weight" to them in terms of our respect. We are to count "heavy" their words, their welfare, their total better interests. To honor them is to give to them that same devotion of heart and life in the human sphere that we give to the LORD in the spiritual sphere, for the Scriptures call upon us to honor both God and our parents. When we honor our parents we count them of supreme worth. Honoring one's parents is, in effect, to measure their value. One recognizes their intrinsic worth because of parenthood, as well as their accumulated worth or value because of the family context which they provide.

To honor one's parents may also be understood from the negative point of view. The statement of curses used in the early tribal confederacy is felt by some to have come from Israel's earliest days. "Cursed be he who *dishonors* his father or his mother" (Deut. 27:16). The literal meaning of the Hebrew word "dishonor" means "to be light, swift, trifling." How vivid is the contrast! Two words sum up quite vividly two possible attitudes toward parents: One, to treat them *lightly;* the other, to treat them *heavily!*

The seriousness with which the Israelite community accepted the Fifth Commandment is clearly revealed in the ascription of the death penalty to cases wherein parents were abused by children. The death penalty was prescribed for cases of striking one's parents (cf. Ex. 21:15); cursing them (cf. Ex. 21:17; Lev. 20:9); or for being generally disobedient and riotous, incorrigible (cf. Deut. 21:18 ff.).

The extremity of such a penalty should not be interpreted as part of the permanent revelation of God. In view of the total revelation of God, it is inconceivable that God would either demand or that any responsible person would agree to the taking of his child's life today, regardless of the disrespect manifested or the lack of honor shown by the child toward the parent. Here, one should distinguish between the cultural practices of the day (the death penalty for disrespect toward one's parents), and the ultimate will of God (parents are to be honored, and disrespect is to be disciplined in keeping with the revelation of God). This practice simply underscores the necessity of dealing with the biblical revelation in terms of principles rather than as a rigid code of unbending law. Or, to refer to the Second Commandment once again, this emphasizes the nature of God's revelation as living word rather than as a rigid form such as characterized the practice of idolatry.

Positive Benefits of the Commandment

As a result of keeping the commandment, Exodus states only "that your days may be long in the land which the LORD your

God gives you." Length of life was considered the sign of God's blessing. To "go down to the grave full of years" was the mark of an honored and satisfied life. As the commandment appears in Exodus, there is no element of command in the closing exhortation. Rather, man finds encouragement in the assurance that the quality of his response in the home will be related to the permanence of his own life and efforts.

Deuteronomy, however, not only makes reference to the length of days but adds two other considerations: "As the Lord your God commanded you" and "that it may go well with you." The element of command leaves no doubt concerning the divine attitude toward the relationship of the child to his parents.

In the Old Testament, good fortune was consistently associated with faithful conduct. Although there are limitations to this view, as the book of Job and others demonstrate, godliness does not always bring good fortune in life; neither is good fortune necessarily a sign of divine approval. Yet, it reflects a principle that is true within certain limitations set by the Bible. One should understand, however, that though he practice the commandment faithfully he still may face hardship, misfortune, and disaster, as he is caught up in the events of life with all other men.

The relationship between faithfulness to the Lord and his way of life on the one hand and good fortune or a good society on the other is much like the relationship between the main product and the by-product in industry. There are some things in industry which are quite valuable, which come only as by-products of another process. The industry does not seek first the by-product, but the primary objective. The by-product comes in the outworking of the main process.

So it is with the relationship between faithfulness to the Lord and the good life associated with his service. If we seek first the good life, we will never find it. It comes only as the by-product of another process—our relationship to God. Therefore, if we will concentrate on the primary objective—seeking first the kingdom of God—then, as by-products, many other beneficent attitudes and conditions will emerge.

Contemporary Claims for Unity Within the Family

As God's living word that comes to every generation, demanding response, the Fifth Commandment is a continuing call for unity within the family structure. What may we learn from the commandment which will be of benefit to us in our own struggle for the permanence of the family and the home as the basic unit of society?

First, *unity should be a basic characteristic of the family*. According to the biblical ideal as expressed in the Fifth Commandment, there is an imperishable quality of unity that runs through one generation to another, linking the several generations of a family into a unified whole. Each member of the family is sensitive to the person and needs of others.

"Brokenness" was never intended to characterize the home. Yet, it is one of the primary characteristics of the family today. While the commandment is concerned primarily with the unity that prevailed in the parent-child relationship, the same principle is applicable to all areas of the home. The biblical ideal knows nothing of broken family relationships, whether husband-wife, parent-child, brother-to-brother, or whatever the relationship may have been.

Second, *honor of parents by children is not grounded in parental rights alone but in the express revelation of the* LORD. The commandment does not say, "*If* your parents are honorable, considerate to children, and deserving of respect, *then* children are to honor them." There is a basic area of relationship that irrevocably ties parent to child and child to parent, a relationship which is to manifest honor or respect for parents. Parents have a right to expect this from their children. This does not mean that parents are to expect an unnatural exaltation by their children. It does mean that they have every right to be treated with consideration, respect, love, and equity.

Does this mean that the child of a reprobate is to honor the way that his or her father has followed? Certainly not! Yet, there is a basic responsibility toward the better interests of the parent. At times, one may manifest "honor" by his sense of concern. To reach the point of feeling "I couldn't care less" stands in opposition to the spirit of this commandment. Children who "honor" their parents will never cease to care, even when every action of their parents is an offense to both God and man.

Third, *the commandment originated in an area of adult responsibility*. It becomes more relevant as the span of life increases, and as more and more couples confront their responsibilities to aging parents. When parents become senile, is it "honoring" them to commit them to a mental institution? There is nothing inherently wrong in helping to provide professional care in a home for aged people. But is it an "honor" to parents to push them out into such homes, simply because of their advancing years, clumsy manners at the table, or other attendant problems of old age?

How may we best "honor" our parents? We honor them by showing to them the respect which their very parenthood deserves. We may not always agree with them, but in every instance we can manifest the love, courtesy, and consideration which they deserve. We honor them when we allow the maturity of their counsel to guide us in early years, even as we allow the warmth of their love to show concern in our later years. We honor them in the little things of life: the spoken word of love and appreciation, the letter which maintains the unity of family, or the visit of genuine warmth and love. Such loving honor can be shown by "*obedience* in our younger years, by *support* in their older years, and by *respect* through all the years."[1]

Fourth, *honor should be given to parents while it may be meaningful*. This is not grounded directly in the biblical understanding of the Fifth Commandment. Yet, I cannot refrain from expressing a word of genuine concern and encouragement. Honor your parents while you have occasion to do so and while it may be most meaningful to them. Unless one is careful, life will soon run its course and the deeds that we often thought to do will have remained undone. After your parents are gone, it will do little good to profess your deep honor for them if you never appropriately expressed it before. If you have not honored them in this life, it does not matter how deeply you mourn their passing. Elaborate floral wreaths and a profusion of tears are poor substitutes for respect and honor for your parents while they are with you. While they are physically able to enjoy life, seek to bring the same joy and gladness to their advancing years that they brought to your younger years. Victor Hugo observed that

> A house is built of logs and stone,
> Of tiles and posts and piers;
> A home is built of loving deeds
> That stand a thousand years.[2]

The one word that sums up the Fifth Commandment is UNITY. There is a bond of unity that runs vertically from one generation to another, tying the entire family into one bond. There is also a bond of unity that extends horizontally to forge bonds of concern and love within a single generation. The covenant community knew nothing of brokenness. It was a community of unity and mutual concern.

Notes

1. Robert I. Kahn, *The Ten Commandments for Today* (Garden City, New York: Doubleday & Co., Inc., 1964), p. 63. Italics are mine.
2. Quoted from *Masterpieces of Religious Verse*, ed. by James Dalton Morrison (New York and London: Harper & Brothers, 1948), p. 346.

6
RESPONSIBILITY

Life is a treasured possession, the free gift of God to man. Its mysterious and transient nature produces among the living a deeply protective attitude. Man jealously guards the right to life, praying with the psalmist, "Oh guard my life, and deliver me" (25:20). Consequently, the protection of physical life has been of primary concern from the most ancient times. Every civilization has recognized some limitations on the taking of human life.

The Sixth Commandment says, "You shall not kill" (Ex. 20:13; Deut. 5:17).

Perhaps a more serious consideration of the commandment will reveal principles that are quite relevant and which are likely to be violated by each of us.

Life Is Sacred

The prohibition against murder is grounded in the assumption that life itself is sacred. Life is in some sense related to God and is his gift. If life belongs to God, only God has the right to determine life and death. Man is not free to usurp the prerogatives of God.

The distinction between sacred and profane was much more meaningful to the ancient man than to the modern. Consequently, because life was sacred, ancient man confronted it as an area belonging to the divine which could not be trespassed by man (any more than holy places could be profaned, or violated, by human presence; cf. the holy of holies).

The mystery of life.—In ancient thought the mysterious and the holy were closely linked and were all but inseparable. The more mysterious a phenomenon, the more likely it was that ancient man would ascribe to it the qualities of holiness. This was supremely true of God, and the mysterious always characterized concepts of holiness with regard to him. The same was true, to a lesser degree, of man's life. Life itself was a mysterious quality. It came to be viewed as sacred, for no one could begin to explain its origin or its continuation apart from divine activity.

Elements of mystery and holiness concerning life are reflected in the ancient Hebraic understanding concerning the blood. In primitive times men saw the blood flow out of a person, and then witnessed the death of the individual. Logically, according to their patterns of thought, the life must have been in the blood. Thus, life was equated with the blood; "Only you shall not eat flesh with its life, that is, its blood" (Gen. 9:4). "The life of the flesh is in the blood" (Lev. 17:11). Because the mystery of life, which was itself sacred, was associated with the blood, the blood also was looked upon as holy.

The holiness of blood is reflected in that the primary aspect of Hebraic sacrifice lay in the manipulation of the blood. Because the blood was holy, man was forbidden to eat blood (cf. Lev. 17:12). Every time an animal was slain, care was taken that the blood was handled in such manner as to prohibit the profanation of its sacred character (this is the basis for Kosher food today).

In all that has been said concerning the holiness of the blood, however, it should be remembered that the blood was not holy within itself. It was holy because it was equated with life, which was holy. Life was so holy that blood, in which life resided, could not be treated in a profane manner.

The same element of mystery concerning the life of man was

reflected in Assyrian and Babylonian thought. According to their understanding, man's life began when the god Kingu was executed by the assembly of the gods. Then, through the skill of Ea, man was created from the blood of Kingu for the purpose of serving the gods. The Babylonians and Assyrians were not alone in this, however, and all other creation stories also ascribe the origin of man to some phase of activity by the gods. No culture has escaped the conviction that there is an element of mystery and wonder in man which is traceable only to the gods.

The image of God.—The sanctity of life does not reside solely in the mystery of life. If so, one might disregard the sanctity of life, viewing such holiness as no more than a lack of understanding on the part of man concerning his origin. Ultimately both the sanctity and the inherent worth of life are grounded in the biblical assertion that man was created in the image of God and that the image of God continues to govern the attitudes which one holds toward human personality. Apart from the image of God in man, there is no significant basis either for the sanctity or the worth of the individual life. Remove the image of God and man is only one among several of the animal species. Viewed from the image of God, man attains intrinsic worth as a person and, in addition, deserves consideration in keeping with one's actions toward God.

However one may interpret the first chapter of Genesis, and the statement on the image of God especially, it is an inescapable conclusion that man stands at the height of the created order. Of no other could it be said, "God created . . . in his own image, in the image of God he created him" (Gen. 1:27). There is a connecting link between God and man which is absent in all other forms of creation.

Some feel that the image of God in man was lost because of the experience described in Genesis 3. This does not seem to be the case. For example, in Genesis 9, following the flood narrative, the statement appears, "Whoever sheds the blood of man, by man shall his blood be shed, *for God made man in his own image*" (Gen. 9:6). What is the reason for this early prohibition against shedding the blood of a man? "God made man *in his own image!*" Following the flood, man still had the image of God as the basis for prohibiting murder.

In the teaching of Jesus, the parable of the judgment in Matthew 25 reflects the same idea as found in Genesis 9. Man is to be respected and treated with consideration. "As you did it to one of the least of these my brethren, you did it to me" (v. 40). Both Genesis 9 and Matthew 25 assert that what we do to man, we in some sense have done to God. This does not mean, quite obviously, that man has natural qualities of divinity within him. Such a view would have been inconceivable to the ancient Hebrew. It does mean, however, that since God created man in "his image," whatever we do to man affects the "image of God" —and in one sense, God himself.

Life is to be respected because in some way it is directly linked to God. Man's life is not to be protected because of its intrinsic nature but because man is made in the "image of God." To violate man is to violate the image of God within man. Thus, because of man's creation in the image of God, life is sacred.

Life as a sacred trust of the covenant people.—The prohibition of murder in the Sixth Commandment does not exclude all taking of life. For example, the Old Testament speaks over and over of the death penalty; both for civil and religious offenses. It even provides capital punishment in extreme cases of child disobedience. War is favorably accepted (cf. Deut. 20:1 ff.).

The commandment is concerned with life as a sacred trust to the community within the bonds of the covenant. Ultimately, only God has the prerogatives of life and death, but these prerogatives are mediated through the covenant people. Thus, life may be taken under certain conditions. It was not the purpose of the Sixth Commandment to exclude either capital punishment or war. At the level on which the commandment was given it sought, rather, to take life and death out of the hands of the individual and insure that it would remain in the domain of the covenant people—who, presumably, would ascertain the will of God concerning the death penalty or war.

Developing Attitudes Toward the Commandment

The Sixth Commandment was but one expression of the sanctity of human personality in the sight of God. Throughout both the Old and New Testaments, there were continuing attitudes which developed toward the life of man. Many of these embodied the same essential "word" from God as that found in the Sixth Commandment.

Legislation reflecting the commandment.—Generally, the legal sections of the Old Testament limited the taking of life to the community as opposed to individual acts of revenge. An exception to this was the blood feud as reflected in the laws for the cities of refuge (cf. Deut. 19:1 ff.; Ex. 21:12–14; Num. 35:1 ff.), in which individuals implemented punishment in what at times bordered on a spirit of revenge. Yet, it should be understood that the blood feud dates to an early period in the history of Israel and was not a permanent practice.

In its treatment of cases which involved human life, it is significant to note that the Old Testament distinguished clearly between homicide and murder (cf. Ex. 21:12 f.; Deut. 19:4 f.). It is tempting to conclude that the Sixth Commandment deals with premeditated murder as opposed to "killing" in the more general sense. Indeed, the word that is used in the commandment, *ratsach*, is used of murder in the majority of its usages. Yet, it is also used of unintentional death (cf. Deut. 4:42; 19:3, 4,6; Num. 35:6,11,12; Josh. 20:3,5,6; 21:13,21). In most of these cases, however, the person involved was suspected by the community of having been guilty of what we would term murder today.

There is a more general word for kill (*haragh*) in the Old

Testament. It is used many, many times more frequently than is the word *ratsach*. One could legitimately conclude that *within broad limitations* the word in the commandment is used of "murder," while the other word is used in the more general sense of "kill." If this distinction is maintained, it is clear that the commandment involves premeditated murder, or the like, and does not embrace every type of "killing," such as homicide and the death penalty for capital offenses.

Jesus' larger view of the commandment.—For one who is concerned with the total revelation of God, the attitude of Jesus toward the spirit of the Sixth Commandment is most important. In this regard there are three considerations which are relevant.

First, Jesus took the principle of the commandment and expanded it to include human dignity in its larger sense. In the Sermon on the Mount Jesus clearly illustrated the way in which he sought to go beyond the literal letter of the Law to that higher righteousness which was to characterize his kingdom. He said, for example,

"You have heard that it was said to the men of old, 'You shall not kill; and whoever kills shall be liable to judgment.' But I say to you that every one who is angry with his brother shall be liable to judgment; whoever insults his brother shall be liable to the council, and whoever says, 'You fool!' shall be liable to the hell of fire" (Matt. 5:21–22).

Jesus took the sanctity of life, a sanctity created by the image of God, and upon this principle formulated the concept of human dignity which was so characteristic of his ministry. In Moses' day the sanctity of life and the image of God expressed themselves in the prohibition of murder or the taking of life by an individual as opposed to the covenant community. Jesus went beyond this and said that it was not enough that we not murder our brother or take his life at our own discretion. The higher righteousness demands that we manifest respect for human dignity. No man has a right to belittle the personality of another and treat him as less than a person made in God's image. Whether through uncontrolled anger or abusive and insulting language, no one has the right to profane the sanctity of life.

Second, Jesus reflected the inherent worth of human personality throughout all of his ministry. Men are of more value than "many sparrows" (Matt. 10:31), and the needs of man took precedence over even the religious institutions of the day (cf. the manner in which Jesus healed on the sabbath and allowed his disciples to pluck grain, on the assumption that even the sabbath was made for man and not man for the sabbath). Thus, our Lord left for us a noble example, one that we should follow as we recognize the inherent worth of human personality. All men are created in God's image.

Third, Jesus taught that consideration for the needs of others should be grounded in the awareness that what we do to one another we do to him; what we fail to do for one another, we fail to do for him (cf. Matt. 25:31 ff.). In this assumption, Jesus built upon the same foundational principle as the Sixth Commandment: the sanctity of life, and man as created in the image of God.

The Sanctity of Life and Your Actions Today

Changing times bring changing interpretations of the inherent principle of this commandment. In light of this fact, the question which we face is: "How does the sanctity of life and man as made in the image of God affect our actions in this generation?"

First, *contemporary actions in the area of human relations should recognize the sanctity of life*. Such sanctity is based upon the image of God in man. God is the determining factor in assessing the worth and dignity of human personality. Life is the gift of God. Man is created in the image of God. Because of this, life shares in the holiness of God. Anyone who kills usurps the prerogative of God, acting as if he were God, for all life is God's creation. Such an understanding of life has far-reaching implications for murder, suicide, and accidental death induced through inconsiderate and careless action. Those within the covenant community are responsible for the preservation of life through whatever means available.

The sanctity of life also has its positive implications on an individual basis. If your life is sacred, because of the image of God, then there is a continual responsibility inherent within each person to treat life as a gift of God. This involves the stewardship of life, in the broader aspects of stewardship. We are, indeed, "the temple of God." We "are not our own" (cf. 1 Cor. 6:19 f.). This means that one is not only to refrain from the taking of life, his own or that of another, but that anything of detrimental nature which is done to the body is a violation of the spirit of the commandment. Recent studies on the incidence of lung cancer in heavy smokers should cause many to reconsider the "image of God" within, and the subsequent responsibility for the protection of the body and life. The same could be said of other forms of overindulgence, including food. Anything which is detrimental to the well-being of life is a violation of the spirit of the commandment.

Second, *according to the commandment, life is a communal trust held by the community*. This is not to negate individual action and responsibility, but it is to recognize that in its original context the primary purpose of the commandment lay in removing the taking of life from the individual level and placing it in the hands of the covenant community. The Old Testament insisted that the right of life and death ultimately belonged to God, but in order for this prerogative to become operative in history this right was mediated through the covenant community. In the Old Testament there is never any question concerning the right of the community to take life. Thus, in a real sense, life was held in trust for God by the covenant community.

The community today, therefore, has both positive and negative responsibilities toward its members. Negatively, it is to prohibit the taking of life on the individual level, such action being reserved as the prerogative of the covenant community, acting on behalf of God. Positively, the community is to act in such manner as to advance the interests of its members—members who are made in the image of God and whose lives are therefore sacred. Our generation would do well to learn from the Old Testament the positive and negative aspects of community responsibility toward the individual and to recognize that these are essentially religious responsibilities. The purpose of the covenant community is, in part, to protect the best interests of its members as the community responds to the realization that every person is made in the image of God and therefore is sacred, deserving respect.

Third, *war and capital punishment were not prohibited by the Sixth Commandment*. Appeal is often made to the commandment in opposition to both of these. This is not a legitimate appeal. As pointed out earlier, the Old Testament over and over imposes the death penalty, and war is postively approved in the vast majority of instances.

Having said this, however, one should recognize that the spirit of the commandment should lead us to seek a better solution to both capital punishment and war. In fact, in the idealistic passages of the Old Testament the future is often described in terms of absolute peace and the absence of war (cf. Isa. 2:2 ff.; Mic. 4:1 ff.). Indeed, in such a time no man will worry about those who would harm him. "They shall sit every man under his vine and under his fig tree, and none shall make them afraid" (Mic. 4:4). The spirit of the commandment implies that the goal of the covenant people ought to be the redemption of human personality, not its extinction.

Action concerning war and capital punishment must, of course, be guided by the protection of the community at large. All personality is sacred, and it may well be that in order to insure life for the greatest number, some members of the community must be permanently removed from society in order that the larger good may be protected.

Until such time as it can be demonstrated with clarity that the removal of capital punishment will do nothing to impair the welfare of the larger community, members of the covenant community, the church today, would do well to "go slow" in its absolute insistence that such action is a direct offense against God's will for our era. No one would question the ultimate will of God in this matter; he does not desire the extinction of any life. Many do question whether unredeemed society is capable of reflecting the absolute will of God.

In the intermediate period, prior to the reign of God's absolute will, we would do well to be guided by the realization that while the Scriptures permit capital punishment, it is not obligatory. This should leave enough freedom to move forward in the realization of God's absolute will, the redemption of all personality as opposed to the extinction of personality. It should be equally recognized, however, that capital punishment and war alike may well be, for the total community, the lesser of two evils. It is biblically sound to consider the welfare of the total covenant community in this matter, as opposed to the isolated individual.

Fourth, *Jesus' larger interpretation of the Sixth Commandment lights the path for us.* Some may argue that because of cultural background, including education, many do not reflect a sense of dignity and worth. This is obviously the case. But this does not mean that all men do not have an inherent dignity and worth. The most culturally refined person living outside the redemptive power of God may reflect as little dignity and worth as the most crudely offensive person. In this regard, we should remember the Lord's counsel to Samuel: "The LORD sees not as man sees; man looks on the outward appearance, but the LORD looks on the heart" (1 Sam. 16:7). Can we reject what God accepts?

Human relations would be revolutionized overnight if we took seriously the implications of this commandment. There would be no necessity for Federal legislation, or legislation on any level, if we would simply treat all men in the same manner that we would treat the Son of God! For in a sense, what we do to the Negro, Oriental, or other nonwhite, we do to God, for all men are made in the image of God.

Many of us should ask, not whether we have ever killed anyone, but "how many men have I murdered?" We can kill a man in far more ways than the taking of his physical life. Or at least Jesus insisted that this was the case (cf. Matt. 5:21 ff.). John Calvin Slemp wisely reminds us:

There are other methods of killing a man that are quite as effective as cutting off his head or shooting him. To call him "Raca"—a blockhead, a worthless nobody—and treat him so long enough, is to murder his personality, even though his body is not molested. Pay him a starvation wage, circumscribe his opportunity to live well himself and to make adequate provision for his family, force him into debt and despair, imprison him in an economic system from which he sees no way of escape, cause him to think that so far as the world cares he may as well be dead—*to do this is to murder the man in the man*.[1]

The letter of the Law insists that no individual has the right to take the life of another; this is reserved as a prerogative of God, mediated through the covenant community. We are, therefore, to avoid the taking of human life through any imaginable method.

The spirit of the Law goes far beyond this. It insists that life is sacred—the gift of God—that man is created in the image of God. The commandment may be summed up in one word—RESPONSIBILITY. Life is a sacred trust to the individual and to the community. Both are ultimately responsible to God.

For many of us the Golden Rule has been held up as a noble example, worthy of practice. "Do unto others as you would have them do unto you." Yet, this is a rather limited view of life. Indeed, there is a sense in which it is a self-centered, selfish standard. What have we done when we do *only* what *we* would want done for *us?*

There is a higher way of life. Traces of it appear in this commandment. It emerges "full blown" in the words of our Lord. Let us build upon his higher interpretation of the commandment and formulate a new standard of conduct in human relations, a standard that will take seriously the image of God in man and the inherent dignity and worth of every person.

Are not those who have known the redemptive power of our Lord under this higher righteousness to "do unto others as you would do unto your Lord"? "For as you did it to one of the least of these my brethren, you did it to me." This is God's word within the words of the commandment.

Notes

1. John Calvin Slemp, *Twelve Laws of Life* (Philadelphia: The Judson Press, 1950), p. 55. Italics are mine.

7
FIDELITY

The eroding effects of adultery have scarred and corroded every generation. "He who commits adultery has no sense; he who does it destroys himself" (Prov. 6:32). The problem of adultery became so serious by the time of Jeremiah that he characterized the men of his day as "well-fed lusty stallions, each neighing for his neighbor's wife" (Jer. 5:8). If the bluntness of Jeremiah's description offends the delicate senses of the reader, one should remember, first, that the prophets spoke at times with an all-but-crude forthrightness which left no doubt in the mind of the hearer concerning the action described (cf. Jer. 2:23 ff.; Ezek. 16:1 ff.; Hos. 4:13 f.). Second, although the prophet's crude expression may be offensive, it is far too accurate a description to be either denied or ignored.

"You shall not commit adultery" (Ex. 20:14; Deut. 5:18).

The relevance of the Seventh Commandment should be readily apparent to those in touch with contemporary society. Extramarital sexual relations have at times been justified on the assumption that only through such permissive "variety" could the original marriage be maintained. Accounts of suburban parties concluded by an exchange of house keys—and wives—have been frequent enough to demand some acceptance of their reality.

A youthful and very lovely Christian bride sincerely sought help in a public question-and-answer session. She and her husband faced the problem of attempts to involve them in an arrangement whereby marriage partners would be shared. According to her friends, with her "Victorian morals" she was living in another day. When conditions such as these appear in a single community during a limited number of years, there is cause to believe that the situation today is not greatly different from that described by Jeremiah.

The Sanctity of Marriage

Jeremiah's portrait is that of life on the animal level. Many live on this level—"each neighing for his neighbor's wife." But the animal level was intended for animals, not for men! Men made in the image of God were created for a higher way. In the lives of those redeemed by the power of God and transformed into a new creation, life need not be lived on the animal level.

Marriage is a sacred relationship. Those within the covenant community know the certainty of Malachi's assertion that "the LORD was witness to the covenant between you and the wife of your youth" (2:14). When God is made part of the marriage covenant the relationship is lifted from the animal level to that higher level of sanctity and purity envisioned by God for every marriage.

Marriage and religious responsibility.—Although there were no religious ceremonies prescribed in connection with marriage in the Old Testament, marriage was consistently brought within the realm of religious life. The Old Testament knows no "religious" and "nonreligious" distinction. One is to live *all* of life within the will of God.

For example, the primary purpose of the writer of Genesis, especially 2:24–25, was to relate the sexual union of man and woman to the intentional will of God. It was because of God's action in the creation of man and woman that the writer declared, "Therefore a man leaves his father and his mother and cleaves to his wife, and they become one flesh" (Gen. 2:24).

The interpretation of adultery as a violation against the LORD is further evidence that marriage was related to religious levels of interpretation (cf. Abraham and Sarai, Gen. 12:10 ff.; 20:1 ff; Isaac and Rebekah, Gen. 26:1 ff.; David and Bathsheba, 2 Sam. 11:1 ff.). Especially does the inclusion of adultery within the Ten Commandments bring marriage into the sphere of religion. It stood there among the basic responsibilities of the person who entered into covenant with the LORD.

Thus, while there may have been no specifically religious ceremony which characterized marriage in the Old Testament, marriage was viewed in relationship to God. Marital infidelity was consistently brought within the area of divine judgment (cf. Ex. 20:14; Deut. 5:18; Lev. 20:10; 2 Sam. 12:1 ff.; Mal. 3:13 ff.).

Social unity of the family.—The specific mention of adultery was intended to insure the solidarity of the family. It is only by implication that the command may be related to the whole range of sexual morality. The essential purpose of the commandment lay in preserving the family as a social unit, inviolable to any disintegration. The commandment guaranteed the marital rights of the husband, thus insuring the solidarity of marriage.

If the emphasis upon protecting the rights of the husband seems strange, one should remember that, according to ancient thought, a woman did not have full, basic rights as an individual.

For example, a woman was not considered as a participant of the covenant except through her husband. Although her status was often an honored one (cf. Prov. 31:10 ff.), she remained in the complete control of her husband. Even a vow made to the LORD was subject to her husband's approval and could be revoked if he did not agree with it. "If . . . her husband . . . expresses disapproval, then he shall make void her vow which was on . . . her lips, by which she bound herself; and the LORD will forgive her" (Num. 30:8; cf. 30:1 ff.).

Legal sections of the Old Testament concerning sexual violations are grounded in protection of the man's rights and take little, if any, consideration of the wrong done to an assaulted woman. In the assault of a virgin betrothed to an Israelite, the death penalty was to be passed (cf. Deut. 22:22–25). In the case of the assault of a virgin who was not betrothed, the death penalty was not invoked. A fine was paid to the father of the young woman, since the father's rights had been offended (cf. Deut. 22:28 f.). In both cases the law sought to protect the man involved.

Foundational nature of the commandment.—Despite the fact that the commandment was primarily concerned with insuring the rights of the husband and the unity of the family as a social entity, the commandment sets forth other foundational principles of continuing worth.

First, in its insistence that violation of the marital bonds is a sin against the LORD, the commandment assumes the sanctity of marriage as a divine institution, subject to religious interpretation and control. *Second,* the unity of the family is to be guarded against any infringement. The case in point involves adultery. But anything that breaks the unity of the family is also to be avoided. *Third,* both the sanctity of marriage and the unity of the family are bound up in the control of sexual relations by marital bonds. In this regard, the commandment does not pass judgment upon other areas of sexual activity, but it does insist that within the community of the LORD there is to be no violation of the husband-wife relationship by outside intervention.

Strangely, the word "adultery" (*na'aph*) is used quite infrequently in the legal sections of the Old Testament, appearing only in the Ten Commandments (cf. Ex. 20:14; Deut. 5:17), and in Leviticus 20:10. It is mentioned by name four times in the Writings: Proverbs 6:32; 30:20; Job 24:15; and Psalm 50:18. Five of the Prophets use the word, but Isaiah (57:3) and Malachi (3:5) mention it only once. Hosea referred to it by name (4:2; 7:4; 3:1; 4:13,14; 2:4), as did Ezekiel (16:38; 23:45; 23:37; 16:32; 23:43). Yet, it was the prophet Jeremiah who dealt most forcefully with the problem (cf. Jer. 23:14; 7:9; 5:7; 3:8; 9:1; 23:10; 29:23; 13:27).

To understand the commandment, one must know the difference between adultery and fornication.

Adultery in the Old Testament involved extramarital sexual relations; more specifically, the aggression of a male, married or single, against the wife of a fellow Israelite. It was generally assumed that adultery was committed by the male in the sense that he was the aggressor. The woman is also spoken of as an "adulteress," but in a secondary sense only. One should notice the phrasing, "If a man commits adultery with the wife of his neighbor, both the adulterer and the adulteress shall be put to death" (Lev. 20:10).

Technically, there is a slight difference between the Old Testament understanding of adultery and the contemporary attitude. Webster, for example, defines adultery as "sexual intercourse between a married man and a woman not his wife, or between a married woman and a man not her husband." It is highly doubtful that the Old Testament viewed sexual intercourse between a married man and a woman as adultery, unless the woman happened to have been married. Adultery was primarily a violation against the husband of the woman involved.

"Fornication" is defined by Webster as voluntary sexual intercourse between an unmarried woman and a man, especially an unmarried man. This is not a matter for specific consideration by name in Old Testament legal codes. In considering this issue, cases involving a betrothed girl should not be considered, since engagement was synonymous with marriage (although the two certainly did not live together). To violate a virgin betrothed to a man was to commit adultery (in the same context the writer of Deuteronomy 22:23–24 speaks of the same person as a "betrothed virgin" in verse 23, and as "his neighbor's wife" in verse 24). Hence, the death penalty for violating a betrothed virgin rested in the law of adultery.

The word commonly translated "fornication" is *zanah* and literally means to be a harlot or to commit harlotry. It is quite often used in a symbolic manner to portray the infidelity of Israel to the LORD, but such references are of no value to the present discussion. Seldom should *zanah* be understood in the manner in which Webster defines "fornication."

This does not mean that premarital sexual relations were condoned in Israel. They were prohibited. But the legal codes do not include such specific prohibitions except those involving a virgin. It is certain, however, that such conduct was generally disapproved. For example, Amnon's half-sister sought to dissuade him by saying, "No, my brother, do not force me; for such a thing is not done in Israel; do not do this wanton folly" (2 Sam. 13:12). Much earlier, Judah responded to Tamar's sexual relations following the death of her husband Er by saying, "Bring her out, and let her be burned" (Gen. 38:24). Although Tamar's action was spoken of as "harlotry," there is no evidence that she was being judged as a prostitute. The reference is seemingly to sexual relations during the time she was without a husband, Er's brother having failed to fulfil his responsibility toward his brother's widow (cf. Gen. 38:5 ff.).

These distinctions have not been pointed out to leave the impression that fornication was treated lightly in the Old Testament. Exactly the opposite could be argued with equal validity. The absence of legislation may reflect that customs concerning fornication were so rigid no laws were needed to regulate conduct. In addition, the Old Testament did deal with the violation of a virgin, although it did not deal with general promiscuity (cf. Ex. 22:15; Deut. 22:28 ff.).

Early marriages and long-term engagements, during which any violation of the betrothed was considered adultery (cf. Deut. 22:22–27), combined to lessen the problem of premarital sexual relations. It is also quite revealing that sexual relations outside the bounds of marriage, exclusive of adultery, were graphically described with the word *zanah*, meaning to be a harlot or prostitute. However, this does not necessarily imply that the person so described was a professional harlot. For example, Hosea's reference to "your daughters when they play the harlot" (4:14) more likely concerned sexual promiscuity than actual prostitution.

In the Old Testament especially did prostitution and the ordeal reflect the inferior status of woman. In both ancient and modern practices, prostitution severs the sexual relation from the intended purpose of God, reducing it to no more than the animal level of self-gratification. Its accepted practice in early Israel reflected the inferior role of woman, making her no more than an object at the service of man.

The ordeal described in Numbers 5 also indicates woman's inferior role. If even suspected of adultery, the woman could be subjected to the ordeal (which is not far removed in principle from the witch hunts of Puritan Massachusetts or the ordeal described in the Code of Hammurabi). Quite significantly, there is no ordeal prescribed for a man suspected of having committed adultery!

One must understand such passages as cited above as the passing understanding of ancient man, not as the permanent will of God. Otherwise, we will be obligated to practice the ordeal, even as Israel did thousands of years ago!

God always has more to say than any generation can comprehend. This is the reason we do not at times have a higher understanding of God's will within the Old Testament.

Deed and Motivation: A New Testament Consideration

Jesus habitually went beyond the literal letter of the Law. Strangely, he did not do this by abolishing the Commandments but by filling them with new meaning as he sought for the spirit inherent in God's word. He did this in the case of the Seventh Commandment.

Jesus said, "You have heard that it was said, 'You shall not commit adultery.' But I say to you that every one who looks at a woman lustfully has already committed adultery with her in his heart" (Matt. 5:27 f.). Certainly, Jesus did not intend to convey the idea that temptation was equally as wrong as the act. Neither was he suggesting that an evil thought was tantamount to an evil act. He did convey the principle that it was wrong to consider a woman "lustfully." In such cases, one had already committed adultery in his heart, the source of intellect or volitional decision, not the seat of emotion as popularly supposed.

One cannot say with finality why Jesus placed such stress upon the lustful thought. There are, however, three considerations which may be helpful. *First,* Jesus recognized that the way one felt toward another "within his heart" affected the individual himself. No person can constantly give himself to thoughts of immorality and not become emotionally warped. Jesus was, therefore, concerned about the detrimental effects upon the person who harbored such thoughts. Positively stated, Jesus sought to redeem the person guilty of the sin of lust. This is borne out in his later advice: "It is better that you lose one of your members than that your whole body be thrown into hell" (Matt. 5:29). A lustful heart is self-destructive. Jesus sought to deliver man from this quality of destruction.

Second, Jesus condemned an inner attitude of lust because of the direct relationship between motivation and deed. The intention today may become the act tomorrow. James suggests: "Each person is tempted when he is lured and enticed by his own desire. Then desire when it has conceived gives birth to sin; and sin when it is full-grown brings forth death" (James 1:14–15). Purity of action depends upon purity of thought, and the mind filled with imagined immoralities is often but the prelude to the immoral life.

Third, motivation was important in the mind of Jesus because thoughts such as those described by Jesus portray what we genuinely think of other people. To contemplate illicit sexual relationships reveals an intrinsic failure to appreciate fully the dignity and worth of the person. Imagined immoralities are indicative of the true feelings that we have toward those whom we know, men and women, and with whom such affairs are envisioned. Although no one may ever know, other than the individual himself, lustful thoughts betray a lack of appreciation for the dignity and worth of human personality made in the image of God. They portray a failure to appreciate either the husband (wife) whose home is violated, or the woman (man) who is the object of lust.

For you or me to think lustfully of an acquaintance reveals a low estimate of that person; despite all insistence to the contrary. Once the anticipated act is accomplished, this inner lack of appreciation often appears. This was the case in Amnon's seduction of Tamar. Having lusted for her, he finally forced her. "Then Amnon hated her with very great hatred; so that the hatred with which he hated her was greater than the love with which he had loved her. And Amnon said to her, 'Arise, be gone'" (2 Sam. 13:15).

The Word Still Calls

God's Word still calls to us, insisting that for those who are his people there can be but one standard for marriage—absolute fidelity. The one word that sums up the Seventh Commandment is PURITY—purity of thought and of deed in sexual relations.

The Old Testament in the light of the New Testament combines with contemporary problems to give us some continuing principles concerning purity of sexual life applicable to our age.

First, *the sanctity of marriage is a basic assumption of the biblical revelation.* For those within the community of faith, marriage is a holy covenant between the two persons and the LORD. Not every person enters into marriage with this understanding. Such an understanding is born in an experience of grace with the LORD and is nurtured through successive years of fellowship with him.

Second, *the unity of the family was of primary concern to the biblical writer.* Although the Seventh Commandment deals only with adultery as a threat to such unity, the spirit of the commandment opposes all disintegrating elements. It is of especial importance, however, to observe that marital infidelity is a primary factor in breaking the home. Admittedly, there are quite often contributory factors which lead to adultery; infidelity then is symptomatic of other problems. But it continues to remain true that the marriage which can triumph over a series of serious obstacles may eventually fall with the emergence of adultery.

Third, *fidelity to marital bonds is an assumption directly related to the commandment.* It is not sufficient that one not violate his neighbor's marriage, which is the literal intention of the Seventh Commandment. Positively stated, the biblical revelation assumes that one will remain faithful to his own marital covenant. Faithfulness is an absolute prerequisite to the fulfilment of God's will for marriage. Anything less than this, for whatever period of time or for whatever reason, is a rupture of one's covenant with the LORD, the covenant of marriage which was made not only with the marriage partner but with the LORD!

Fourth, *fulfilment of the spirit of the Seventh Commandment demands a sense of respect for human personality.* To violate the marriage of a couple is to manifest gross disrespect for both partners of that marriage. The biblical revelation insists that one should have such honor and respect for his neighbor as to refrain from violating his wife. To violate a man's wife is to treat the husband with contempt. More than this, however, adultery also reflects a total lack of appreciation for the woman involved. Not only in causing her to be unfaithful, but in violating the bonds of marriage, one also treats her with contempt. Many would argue this point to the contrary. Yet, it remains true that the violation of marriage reflects a lack of appreciation for both persons; the husband and wife equally being treated with a sense of contempt which is manifest in the assumption that their person and prerogatives can be manipulated for your pleasure.

Fifth, *sex, according to the biblical ideal, must take into consideration the totality of human personality.* Hebrew thought saw man as a unified whole; physical body and spirit producing a "soul" (which is best understood as a "living, breathing" entity). To exploit sex in isolation from the total personality is to violate this basic, biblical understanding of personality. Prostitution is the most flagrant example of sex isolated from human feelings of warmth and dignity. But premarital and extramarital sexual relations more often than not reflect the same failure to respect the personality of the individual involved. Sex, separated from genuine interest, concern, mutuality, and true love, is no more than the self-centered satisfaction of one's own animal instincts. On the other hand, sex when related to the totality of human personality is the ultimate union of man and woman, a union designed by God himself.

Sixth, *although it took considerable time to do so, the Old Testament eventually apprehended that there was no double standard of morality.* Hosea, in condemning the men of his day said, "I will not punish your daughters when they play the harlot, nor your brides when they commit adultery; for the men themselves go aside with harlots, and sacrifice with cult prostitutes" (4:14). Hosea insisted that the Lord does not condone the manner in which men, then or today, assume that they can live a promiscuous sexual life, all the while expecting that their wives and daughters maintain a higher level. The biblical revelation insists that there is but one standard for sexual conduct: absolute purity, whether for men or for women. In essence, the biblical revelation knows nothing of a "moral holiday," during which either husband or wife, married or unmarried person, is free from the highest biblical understanding of the will of God for sexual relations.

Seventh, *the biblical revelation assumes that sexual life is as legitimate an area for discussion and counsel as is any other area of life.* For example, an investigation of the legal codes of the Old Testament reveals that topics on sex were dealt with forthrightly, and the will of God was portrayed with regard to this aspect of life as to others.

Yet, have we not responded, in many cases, by shunning such discussion? I have known cases in which young people were not allowed to read parts of the Old Testament because of its frank discussion of sexual life, its wholesome side and its perversions. Do we really believe it possible, or desirable, to create a vacuum in which we rear our children? What happens when the vacuum is gone? What principles do they have by which to make their own decisions?

If we would let the Scriptures speak with unique frankness concerning the sanctity of marriage, and of sex, as well as the abhorrent nature of sexual perversions (cf. Lev. 18:6 ff.; 20:10 ff., and examples from the historical materials), much could be accomplished in stemming the current degenerate emphases on sex which plague our children. Many have taken the attitude that sex education should be avoided, and this has far too often included sex education in the home as well as public areas of instruction. But those who deny the legitimacy of such counsel may be sure that sex education is being carried out—tragically, too often, through the contemporary movie, novel, sensational magazine, or the crudities scrawled on a thousand walls and public rest rooms in any city!

Our decision is not whether sex education will be given, but who will give it, and whether it will be given from the perspective of the biblical revelation (not even the most up-to-date sociological interpretation of sex will substitute for a religious interpretation). Let us allow the total Bible to speak to the total person! Who are we to determine what and to whom it shall be allowed to speak?

8
HONESTY

"The real significance of crime," said Joseph Conrad, "is in its being a breach of faith with the community of mankind." This succinct appraisal well summarizes the principle inherent within commandments six through ten. Through violating the rights of other covenant members, one breaks faith with the spirit of the covenant, and in turn with the community.

Commandment Eight says, "You shall not steal" (cf. Ex. 20:15; Deut. 5:19).

In considering the Eighth Commandment, one should recognize, therefore, that theft is essentially a breach of faith with the covenant community. The community has every right to assume that members respect the rights of others concerning the possession of property.

Those who are bound together in covenant should be able to trust one another. God desires the creation of a community wherein men need not fear theft. Ideally, the kingdom of God is a "kingdom with no keys" (but don't leave the keys in your car when you leave it—not quite yet!).

Property Rights in the Ancient Near East

Many centuries before the time of Moses, nations of the ancient Near East formulated codes of law to regulate conduct.

During the first half of the nineteenth century B.C., Lipit-Ishtar, in the prologue of his law code, summarized the purpose of his kingship: "To establish justice in the land, to banish complaints, to turn back enmity and rebellion by the force of arms, (and) to bring well-being to the Sumerians and Akkadians."[1]

Later, Hammurabi declared that his selection by the gods was "to cause justice to prevail in the land, to destroy the wicked and the evil, that the strong might not oppress the weak, to rise like the sun over the black-headed (people), and to light up the land." Later, he said, "I established law and justice in the language of the land, thereby promoting the welfare of the people."

In view of this purpose, it is hardly surprising that property rights were of fundamental importance in ancient codes of law.

Basic view of property.—The extensive and detailed manner in which the Code of Hammurabi deals with theft reflects the fundamental importance of property rights in the ancient world. Other codes reflect the same concern. An examination of his code reveals that property rights, including interest payments, rental agreements, and other matters related to property, constitute the greatest single area of concern in the law code.

Many feel that violations of property were in some sense viewed as a violation of the person. J. Pedersen has suggested:

As for property, this principle [i.e. encroachment of property as a matter of family honor] has been maintained to the largest extent by the Arabians, with whom the infringement of property is always a breach of honour demanding satisfaction; and this close connection between man and property is still recognized by the eastern Semites who react violently against every encroachment on property.[2]

Severity of penalties.—In the laws of Hammurabi the death penalty is normally passed in cases of theft. Even in the case permitting restitution, the amount of indemnification (as high as thirty times the value of the property) is so exorbitant that escape from the death penalty is all but impossible.

Assyrian laws of the twelfth century B.C. (this is the date for the tablets; the laws go back to the fifteenth century B.C.) prescribe bodily mutilation for cases of theft. This involved cutting off an ear, or, on occasion, the nose. If a slave, for example, received stolen property from the owner's wife, both the nose and ears of the slave were cut off. If a man's wife stole property valued at over five minas of lead her husband could ransom her, but was obliged to cut off her ears. If her husband did not ransom her, the neighbor could cut off her nose. In the case of a man who encroached on his neighbor's "more important bounded property," "he shall "give up one-third as much field as he encroached on; they shall cut off one finger of his; they shall flog him one hundred (times) with staves (and) he shall do the work of the king for one full month." The failure to mutilate the face of a man may reflect his superior status in the ancient world.

Babylonian laws.—In cases of theft and robbery during the time of Hammurabi, the death penalty was almost universally applied. "If a seignior stole the property of church or state, that seignior shall be put to death; also the one who received the stolen goods from his hand shall be put to death" (6); "If a seignior committed robbery and has been caught, that seignior shall be put to death" (23). In the case of the theft of animals, restitution to the extent of thirtyfold could be made if they belonged to the state; tenfold if to an individual. Yet, "if the thief does not have sufficient to make restitution, he shall be put to death" (8). If this seems unduly severe one should recall that "in eighteenth-century England there were two hundred offenses punishable by death, including stealing in a shop to the value of five shillings." [3]

The Old Testament View of Property

That property rights had unique significance for Israel is clear in the account of Naboth's vineyard (cf. 1 Kings 21:1 ff.). Not even the king could legitimately confiscate the property of an Israelite landowner. Ahab's offer to give Naboth a better vineyard, or its value in money, eliminates the element of financial injustice as the reason for Naboth's refusal to part with his vineyard. Despite the willingness of the king to trade a better piece of ground, Naboth refused. "The LORD forbid that I should give you the inheritance of my fathers" (1 Kings 21:3). The property was so uniquely related to the family of Naboth that to have forsaken the property would have denied his corporate existence with his family. Property was a part of the person.

Divine ownership.—The Old Testament recognized that the LORD was sole owner of the land. Whether divine ownership extended to personal items of property is questionable, but it is quite likely that in the highest sense *all* property was viewed either as the possession or the gift of the LORD. The land is spoken of as the "land of the LORD" (cf. Hos. 9:3; also Psalm 85:1; Jer. 16:18). The LORD conquered the land and gave it to his people (cf. Num. 32:4; Josh. 23:3,10; 24:11–13). Thus, it was upon the basis of the property right of the LORD that the law of Jubilee was prescribed (cf. Lev. 25:23). As DeVaux well summarizes,

> It is also *in virtue of God's supreme dominion that religious law limits the rights of the human occupants:* hence the duty of leaving gleanings of corn and vines for the poor (Lev. 19:9–10; 23:22; Deut. 24:19–21; cf. Ruth 2); the right of every passer-by to satisfy his hunger when passing through a field or a vineyard (Deut. 23:25–26); the annual tithe due to Yahweh (Lev. 27:30–32), to be eaten in Yahweh's presence (Deut. 14:22–27), given to the Levites (Num. 18:21–32); the tithe every third year for the poor (Deut. 14:28–29; 26:12–15), and the law about the fallow ground in the sabbatical year (Ex. 23:10–11; Lev. 25:2–7).[4]

God was the owner of the land. Israel held property in trust for the LORD. The psalmist captured this emphasis as he exalted God's independence of man's sacrifice: "Every beast of the forest is mine, the cattle on a thousand hills. I know all the birds of the air, and all that moves in the field is mine. If I were hungry, I would not tell you; for the world and all that is in it is mine" (50:10-12).

The sanctity of property.—One is hesitant to speak of the holiness of property. Yet, if one will remember that holiness is a relationship more than it is an attribute, then perhaps it will not appear strange. If property belongs to God, it enters into the category of the sacred as opposed to the profane. Sanctity, or holiness, means separation to or for the service of one's God. In this sense property is holy: it belongs to the LORD and is to be treated accordingly.

The idea of separation involved in sanctity, or holiness, reveals itself in a second way concerning property. Personal property assumed a degree of sanctity, although on the human level, in that it was set aside for the use of a particular person. That which was absolutely holy because it belonged to God came to share characteristics of holiness as men served as stewards of that property.

Penalties for violation of property rights.—Although Israel viewed property seriously, she did not assess the extreme penalties for theft and robbery that other cultures implemented. Mutilation was not practiced by Israel as it was by the Assyrians of the fifteenth to twelfth centuries B.C.; and the death penalty, so frequently imposed in Babylon, was not generally implemented in cases of theft and robbery.

In this regard, the laws of Israel were much closer in spirit to the Hittite laws which manifest greater consideration than Assyrian and Babylonian law codes. In both Hittite and Israelite law codes, restitution and indemnification were allowed to replace the death penalty or mutilation as punishment for crimes of theft or robbery.

Capital punishment for crimes of property was reserved for only the more serious cases. For example, death was the penalty for stealing a man (for the purpose of slavery in all probability); "Whoever steals a man, whether he sells him or is found in possession of him, shall be put to death" (Ex. 21:16). A thief slain during the night did not bring guilt upon his slayer, but during the day his life could not be taken; "If a thief is found breaking in, and is struck so that he dies, there shall be no bloodguilt for him; but if the sun has risen upon him, there shall be bloodguilt for him" (Ex. 22:2–4).

In other cases involving property, whether theft or the abuse of property through negligence, restitution was the general practice (cf. Ex. 22:5–6,14), although at times double restitution was demanded as a penalty (cf. Ex. 22:9). In addition, there were occasions when five times the value was assessed as the penalty for having misappropriated an object (cf. the case of an ox that could not be returned alive, Ex. 22:1).

Continuing Implications

There are several foundational principles that have continuing implications for covenant life.

First, *the sanctity of property* is assumed throughout the Old Testament. This is a strange emphasis for those of us who live in a world sharply divided into the sacred and the profane. Property is normally considered "profane." Yet, for the ancient mind, even property was sacred because it was directly related to God. All cultures recognized that property which had been specifically dedicated was holy to the God or gods, but Israel made a significant advance upon this premise. She concluded that because it was the gift of God, all property was in some sense sacred.

Second, *property is God's to give, not man's to steal*. If all property is the gift of God, then to manipulate property through theft is to usurp the prerogative of God. The LORD makes adequate provision for his own, insuring that, within the limitations imposed by society, his bounty will be shared with all men. To attempt to secure one's own interests through usurping what the LORD has placed in trust with another is a greater sin against the LORD than against one's brother. The bestowal of life's goods, according to biblical thought, is God's to bestow, through the channels which he establishes. It is not man's prerogative to decide whether possessions held by his brother may become his. In essence, there is a sense in which theft is a violation of the sovereignty of God; an attempt to usurp the prerogatives of the LORD by determining what shall and what shall not be yours, rather than leaving this to the outworking of his grace.

Third, *if property is the gift of God, man should be concerned not only to protect his own property but to bring others to know the bounty of the* LORD's *blessing.*

Admittedly, all theft would not disappear, regardless of the adequacy of life's blessing. The possessive instinct is perhaps too strong. As J. Edgar Park suggests, "The stars are in their ancient places simply because they are out of the reach of predatory hands." [5]

Yet, it should be equally obvious that theft often originates in the socially oppressed individual who, because of environmental circumstances, has never known the bounty of others. Nor, in many cases, has he known the quality of home life which others have enjoyed, to say nothing of a vital religious experience. This is not to make excuse, nor to state that many individuals from comparable backgrounds have not proven by their lives that life need not be lived on such a level. But it is to say that we are hardly justified in condemning the thief, unless we can be sure that we have not contributed to the conditions which produced the violation.

Fourth, *corporate theft is equally as serious as individual theft.* There are many, many individuals today who would not think of stealing from an individual, but who think nothing at all of stealing from a corporation, the government, or some other institution. Well do I remember the shame that came to a rather prominent church member when inspectors from his company suddenly "swooped down" and found the way in which he was converting company equipment to his own use. With all honesty, he insisted that he had not stolen anything. He was merely "using" the equipment—although it had been removed from company premises. The tragedy is that the man actually did not consider this as stealing. Neither did most of the leaders in business circles of the community. But is it any worse to steal from an individual than it is to raid the tool bin at Ford, TWA, or some government project? Does the indefinable form of big businesses mean that it is legitimate to steal from them because they are not "persons"?

There is another side to corporate theft; the manner in which the corporation or government develops the attitude that it is "above moral principle." Was Ambrose Bierce's definition of a corporation correct—"An ingenious device for obtaining individual profit without individual responsibility"? Has the corporation stolen from you when it passes off shoddy merchandise, designed to last only slightly beyond the guaranty period? Does the Legislature or the Congress violate the spirit of the commandment when it squanders your tax dollar on political patronage and other vote-getting gimmicks designed, not for the common good, but to insure an adequate number of votes to keep a politician in office? Is it stealing to manipulate the rise and fall of market prices, robbing the individual—who is powerless to alter the situation? Does the financial institution break the commandment when its true rate of interest, as compared with what most people think they are paying, soars to astronomical heights—yet, the wage earner can only "take it or leave it"? Each of these questions should be answered affirmatively. For there is a form of corporate theft, and it is just as reprehensible as a masked robber who stands across the counter and demands the day's receipts at the corner grocery.

Fifth, *there are both tangible and intangible forms of theft.*

Obviously, the Eighth Commandment deals only with the theft of tangible property. Yet, are there not forms of theft which deal primarily with the intangible? Is the person who "goofs off" on the job being honest? Rather, is he not practicing a form of thievery? If we are to fulfil the spirit of the commandment, is it not obligatory upon each of us to give a full day's work for a full day's pay? The opposite is also true—a full day's pay for a full day's work. Does the technical exemption from the minimum wage law exempt an institution, even church-related, from paying wages commensurate with the work done and the needs for basic requirements that exist in an inflationary era? Is it stealing to travel away from home and upon arrival call yourself at your home phone, as many do, thereby notifying your wife or husband that you have arrived safely? All of these are possible. Intangible theft is as serious in the sight of God as the tangible.

E. W. Howe once observed that many a man is saved from being a thief by finding everything locked up. How much better it would be if each of us could be saved from being a thief by following the will of God.

There is one word that sums up this commandment—HONESTY!

Notes

1. *Ancient Near Eastern Texts*, ed. J. Pritchard (Princeton: Princeton University Press, 1950). All citations of ANE sources included are taken from this collection. When specific laws are cited, the numerical designation is based on *Ancient Near Eastern Texts*.

2. Johannes Pedersen, *Israel*, I–II (London: Oxford University Press, 1946), 405.

3. Robert I. Kahn, *The Ten Commandments for Today* (Garden City, New York: Doubleday & Co., Inc., 1964), p. 76.

4. R. DeVaux, *Ancient Israel* (New York: McGraw-Hill Book Co., Inc., 1961), p. 165. Italics are mine.

5. "Exodus," *The Interpreter's Bible*, I (Nashville: Abingdon Press, 1952), 988.

9
INTEGRITY

False witnesses were no strangers to the courts of ancient Israel. Their bruising and destructive testimony was often present. This is reflected in the words of the wise man who said, "A man who bears false witness against his neighbor is like a war club, or a sword, or a sharp arrow" (Prov. 25:18). The author may have fallen into misfortune through a faithless witness. At least he expresses personal insight into such a person: "Trust in a faithless man in time of trouble is like a bad tooth or a foot that slips" (25:19). Anyone who would swear falsely against a neighbor was not then, nor is he today, worthy of the confidence which ideally is to mark members of the covenant community.

"You shall not bear false witness" (cf. Ex. 20:16; Deut. 5:20).

More often than not, the Ninth Commandment is interpreted to refer to truth in all of our relations. Accordingly, the commandment expresses the inherent right of covenant members to expect the truth from one another in human relations. This is a noble emphasis. Yet, in its original context, was the commandment so broad in its scope? Did it speak of truth in *all* human relationships, or was it limited to the more formal area of false testimony?

While the commandment does leave room for the emphasis upon the nobility of truth in the more general sense, it would seem that the primary concern is with the court of law, or other formal or semiformal hearings. If this is the case, then the most important law code of ancient Israel, the Ten Commandments, nobly upholds the sanctity of the court for the stability of the covenant community.

Understanding the Commandment

Literally, Exodus states, "You shall not begin to answer against your neighbor a false witness." Deuteronomy states, "[Neither] shall you begin to answer against your neighbor an empty (false) witness." Perhaps a literal translation of the Hebrew text and an examination of the specific words involved will clarify the issue.

For our specific purposes, the crux of the issue is the word "answer," *'anah*. What does it mean?

Basically, it means to answer, respond. It is a common word in the Old Testament, occurring 316 times. In most instances it means simply to answer or respond to something said, either actual or implied. It is used of both man and God. There are, however, twenty-two occasions when the word is used in the more restricted sense of responding as a witness, or "to testify."[1]

For those who have time to do so, an examination of each of the usages of the word as "to testify" will serve to clarify the meaning of the commandment (cf. Mal. 2:12; 1 Sam. 12:3; 2 Sam. 1:16; Isa. 3:9; 59:12; Mic. 6:3; Neh. 14:7; Job. 15:6; Num. 35:30; Ruth 1:21; Hos. 5:5; 7:10; Job 16:8; 9:14–15; Deut. 5:17; 31:21; 19:16, 18; Ex. 20:16; 23:2; Prov. 25:18).

Thus, while the word means no more than "answer" or "respond" in the vast majority of cases, there is a significant usage of the word with the meaning "to testify." English translations make this quite clear. Samuel, in making his farewell speech to Israel, defends his judgeship by saying, "Here I am; *testify* (*'anah*) against me" (1 Sam. 12:3). Isaiah said, "Their partiality *testifies* against them" (3:9); later, "our sins *testify* against us" (Isa. 59:12). Deuteronomy uses the verb to describe the penalty imposed on the false witness in a court of law (cf. Deut. 19:16,

18). Proverbs 25:8 refers specifically to "a man who *bears* false witness." Exodus 23:2 uses the word also: "You shall not follow a multitude to do evil; nor shall you *bear witness* in a suit, turning aside after a multitude, so as to pervert justice."

Reference to "witness."—In addition to the above evidence, one should consider the use of *'edh*, or witness, which appears in both forms of the commandment. Usually the word refers to testimony given in court and in civil and social relations. Thus, one could translate the commandment, "answer or testify as a false witness against." [2] The action envisioned in the commandment involves one who serves in the capacity of a *witness* in a somewhat technical sense. In this sense it differs from the general gossip described, for example, in Psalm 15:3b.

The "false" witness in Exodus and Deuteronomy.—Both Exodus and Deuteronomy agree in characterizing the witness as "false." But it should be noted that the two forms of the commandment use two different words which are consistently translated in English translations as though they were the same. Exodus uses the word *shaqer*, while Deuteronomy uses the word *shaw'* (the same word that appears in the Third Commandment as "vain").

The word *sh-q-r* has the root meaning "deceive," and in Assyrian means "a lie." The noun in Hebrew has the common meaning "deception, disappointment, falsehood." Whatever deceives, disappoints, and betrays one is spoken of as a *sheqer;* for example, a molten image (cf. Jer. 10:14). The word also means deceit, fraud, or wrong. Particularly is it used of injurious falsehood in testimony, especially in courts. The word is also used of those who prophesy falsely (cf. Jer. 14:14; 23:25–26). At times the word may mean a lie, falsehood, generally (cf. Psalm 101:7; Prov. 13:5; 17:4; Job 36:4).

The use of *shaw'* has already been discussed in the chapter on the Third Commandment. The literal meaning of the word is "emptiness" or "nothingness." A matter is false if it is empty, devoid of content. Often today one hears the colloquial expression, "There's nothing to it."

Both Deuteronomy and Exodus sought to convey the same idea, but they did so through the use of different words. The word used in Exodus more nearly compares to the English word "false," or a "lie," while the word in Deuteronomy means "false" only in a derived sense.

To the discerning person, this should say something concerning the means by which the Bible came to us, and the method of inspiration generally. Both forms of the commandment convey the same message from God, but they do so through completely different word forms. It was not necessary that parallel statements in the Bible be dictated to the biblical writers in exactly the same form, so long as the divine content of the message got through to the reader, or hearer in the case of the spoken word. The essential message of God is the same, whether one translates the commandment "false" or "empty."

In summary, the Ninth Commandment was concerned primarily with false testimony in formal cases, not with cutting gossip of a personal nature, although such gossip may violate the spirit of the commandment. In relating the commandment to a "court," one should be cautious lest he conceive of "court" in the same sense as our modern juristic system. For ancient Israel, the "court" was in many cases the assembly of the elders who gathered at the city gate, or tribal leaders who heard complaints. Later, it may have involved the judges and formal courts of the monarchy. But whatever the specific nature of the authoritative body, the commandment was concerned with a formal hearing at which false testimony might be given against one's neighbor.

The Old Testament Quest for Justice in Legal Procedure

Every possible step was taken in the Old Testament to insure that the system of law would remain just. Despite the temporary breakdown of the courts (cf. Mic. 3:9 ff.; Amos 2:6 ff.; 5:12; 6:1 ff.; 1 Kings 21:8 ff.), Israel's sincere effort to establish an equitable juristic system is a continuing challenge to those who would relate religious commitment to the legal decisions necessary for a stable society.

The principle of justice.—From the beginning of Israel's occupancy of the land she was to "appoint judges and officers in all your towns . . . and they shall judge the people with righteous judgment" (Deut. 16:18). Three principles were to characterize judicial processes: (1) men were not to "pervert justice," (2) they were to show no partiality, and (3) they were not to take a bribe (cf. Deut. 16:19).

Partiality was to be shown to neither rich nor poor. Justice, and only justice, was to be the determining factor within the courts.

Multiple witnesses.—The Ninth Commandment was further strengthened by an insistence that no person could be condemned on the evidence of a single witness. In cases of murder the murderer was to be put to death, but he could not be put to death except on the testimony of multiple witnesses (cf. Num. 35:30). Deuteronomy specifies that the death penalty would be on the evidence of "two witnesses or of three witnesses" (17:6). In addition, "a single witness shall not prevail against a man for any crime or for any wrong in connection with any offence that he has committed; only on the evidence of two witnesses, or of three witnesses, shall a charge be sustained" (Deut. 19:15).

Integrity of a single witness.—The Old Testament constantly appeals for integrity on the part of witnesses. "You shall not join hands with a wicked man, to be a malicious witness. You shall not follow a multitude to do evil; nor shall you bear witness in a suit, turning aside after a multitude, so as to pervert justice; nor shall you be partial to a poor man in his suit" (Ex. 23:1-3).

Proverbs contrasts the faithful and false witness. "A faithful witness does not lie, but a false witness breathes out lies" (14:5). "A false witness will not go unpunished, and he who utters lies will not escape" (19:5). The determinative value of a witness was also clearly recognized; "A truthful witness saves lives, but one who utters lies is a betrayer" (14:25).

Malicious witnesses.—From time to time there no doubt arose men in Israel who were false witnesses, like those messengers of Jezebel who testified falsely against Naboth in order that Naboth's vineyard might be taken from him and given to Ahab (cf. 1 Kings 21:8–14). Deuteronomy had a rather effective, although harsh, manner of dealing with such persons. "If the witness is a false witness and has accused his brother falsely, then you shall do to him as he had meant to do to his brother" (19:18 f.). Thus, a malicious witness in a murder trial would be put to death. Or, in a lesser crime, he would bear the same penalty that would have been passed upon the accused, had the false testimony of the malicious witness been accepted.

It is in this regard that Deuteronomy uses the well-known proverbial saying, "It shall be life for life, eye for eye, tooth for tooth, hand for hand, foot for foot" (19:21). In this context the proverb does not have the harsh overtones often ascribed to it. The writer simply proposes that malicious witnesses should be treated in the same manner that they sought to treat the accused. Such a response does not seem unreasonable.

Witness to participate in execution.—Another aid to maintaining integrity on the part of witnesses was the law which insisted that a witness had to participate in the execution of a condemned person. "The hand of the witnesses shall be first against him to put him to death, and afterward the hand of all the people" (Deut. 17:7). While the specific crime in the context was that of worshiping a foreign god, it may be assumed that the same practice concerning the participation of the witness prevailed in other cases which involved the death penalty.

Arbitration.—The Old Testament recognized the local community as the area where decisions should be reached concerning its own cases. It also recognized, however, that there might arise cases wherein it would be impossible to reach agreement concerning either the nature of the charges or the penalty to ascribe in a particular case. When the local community could not decide its own cases satisfactorily, such cases were submitted to arbitration by a higher court.

> If any case arises requiring decision between one kind of homicide and another, one kind of legal right and another . . . any case within your towns which is too difficult for you, then you shall arise and go up to the place which the LORD your God will choose, and coming to the Levitical priests, and to the judge . . . you shall consult them, and they shall declare to you the decision (Deut. 17:8–9).

This system approximated our present courts of appeal and the concept of the Supreme Court, a source of final appeal.

Obedience to the court decision.—There was no doubt about the binding nature of law in the Old Testament. Every precaution was taken to insure that justice would be carried out on the local level. In cases where there was indecision on the local level, provision was made for an appeal to a higher court. But once the decision had been reached by the final source of authority, obedience to the court was obligatory.

> You shall be careful to do according to all that they direct you; . . . you shall not turn aside from the verdict which they declare to you, either to the right hand or to the left. The man who acts presumptuously, by not obeying the priest who stands to minister there before the LORD your God, or the judge, that man shall die. . . . And all the people shall hear, and fear, and not act presumptuously again (Deut. 17:10–13).

The biblical revelation knows nothing of obeying only those laws that seem good. Especially is this true when there is an orderly procedure for moving from the local to the higher level through the courts in seeking the best solution to a particular legal question. There can be no responsible society built upon an irresponsible attitude toward the law and court decisions. Both the Old and New Testaments agree in demanding observance of the law from citizens of the covenant community.

The Ninth Commandment in the Twentieth Century

In view of the contemporary clash between various racial and social groups with the courts, the principles of the Ninth Commandment are exceedingly relevant. Not only in the more limited sense of bearing honest testimony, but in that larger sense of the integrity of the juristic system, the ninth of God's "ten words" speaks to issues that demand answer in our time.

First, *the principle of truth in all of human relations is foundational* for the commandment. Although the commandment is concerned specifically with the matter of bearing testimony in an official capacity within the community, it is grounded in the broader principle that truth is to characterize the life of those within the covenant community. Those who experience the redeeming power of the LORD are to reflect "truth of word, truth of life, and truth of thought."[3] One's word is to be true and dependable, worthy of trust and confidence by all men.

Truth of life is also to characterize members of God's community.

> Truth and trust form the foundations of society, when society is worthy of the name . . . If by our silence we are creating false impressions, we have already outstepped the limits of truth. If through cowardice we fail to avow our sentiments on the right occasions, we become also the slaves of our fears: we loose our self-respect and foster baseness in our characters. On the other hand, by avowing our convictions and translating them into concrete deeds we strengthen both ourselves and our convictions.[4]

Also, the quest for truth of thought is, or should be, an uppermost concern of the covenant community. Truth of thought is foundational to all other areas of truth. If a man is not true to himself, if he does not know and appreciate the truth at the very inner core of his being, it is highly improbable that he will ever embody either truth of word or truth of life.

The people of God, above all other people, should engage in a continuing search for truth. Whether in intellectual pursuits, biblical study, doctrine, church practices, or individual responses to life, truth cannot conceivably be detrimental to the covenant community. Indeed, the community of faith cannot long survive in the darkness of falsehood and misunderstanding.

The revelation of God has no fear of the light. Rather, the kingdom of our LORD welcomes the light of truth, whatever the corner into which that light may fall. There is no need to feel that the revelation of God must be protected from the truth, whatever the tensions or difficulties precipitated by its appearance. Be sure that you have found truth; then rest with confidence in the assurance that truth can never be incompatible with the revelation of God.

Second, *the juristic system is an expression of the will of God for the community of faith.* Not only in the commandment, but throughout the entire biblical revelation, the juristic system is not only tolerated but positively endorsed. Such endorsement of the court by the biblical revelation rests in the assumption that law and order are prerequisites to the quality of stability in society which is conducive both to the welfare of man as an individual, and to the fulfilment of God's purposes within society. Whether it be an ancient Jewish court, the courts of Rome, or contemporary local, state, or federal courts in this land, all are expressions of the fundamental will of God.

Obviously this does not mean that every decision of a court will be right, nor that it will reflect the will of God. Not even in Israel was this the case. But the principle of divine approval does mean that, as a system, courts find uncompromising approval within the biblical revelation.

Third, *the integrity of individual members of the covenant community* is assumed by the commandment. There is no place for duplicity and dishonesty, whether in word or deed, on the part of those who are members of the community of faith. One is expected to tell "the truth, the whole truth, and nothing but the truth." Members of the covenant community are not only expected to refrain from falsehood, they are actively to seek the truth. We have not fulfilled the full spirit of the commandment when we merely refrain from falsehood, whether in court or other areas of life. The truth is to be sought and then shared by all those who know the LORD.

Fourth, *which laws are we to obey?* There was a time when courts and the juristic system held such respect in this nation that the question of which laws to obey would have been irrelevant. This is no longer true.

Civil rights has brought into clear focus the issue of the Christian's attitude toward the courts of the land. Obviously, there have been disagreements concerning the wide variety of legislation passed and court decrees handed down. The vast majority of the nation has obviously supported both the legislators and the courts. Others have not. The very disagreement, however, affords an excellent laboratory for an examination of the role of the court in the community of faith.

The courts and the legal system have been violated by both extremes. Some have used the complexity of legal machinery to deny voting rights and other basic civil liberties. Issues are often lost not in the decree given but in the years required to go through the courts. In other instances there have been those who have openly defied the orders of the court or legislative body.

We have witnessed the strange emergence of "civil disobedience" in our time; the assumption that if one is willing to pay the penalty, "unjust" laws may be violated without violation of conscience or of basic morality. Such an attitude has an element of justification.

Looking at both of these attitudes, one should then ask, "Can any nation long endure with such an attitude toward the orderly processes of law?" Did not the biblical writer manifest a far better way? He suggested that the local community should settle its own cases, but in difficult matters the higher court would be called upon to render a decision. Then, regardless of one's personal attitude toward the decision, the court was to be obeyed (cf. Deut. 17:8 ff.).

Perhaps the most serious objection to "civil disobedience" is not to the act itself but to the contempt for law that such an attitude brings. Will the youth of the land, or of a particular community, respect the law in the face of such disobedience? Which laws are "unjust"? Who is to decide the matter of justice, once this is removed from the juristic system? Is every man to "do what is right in his own eyes"? This is anarchy, not freedom!

If the disobedience of the law and the willing acceptance of punishment were the only alternatives the issue would be entirely different. But in a nation such as ours, where lawmakers and courts have done more to promote human rights in the past decade than in the entire history of the judicial system—except for the 1860s, perhaps, it is strange to find such basic contempt for law and order. One could argue, of course, that civil disobedience, riots, and other disorders have created a climate in which action has been hastened in granting full civil rights. Mob action, riots, and general disorder no doubt did cause politicians to take more rapid action. Yet, it should never be forgotten that the courts were already moving firmly in this direction. The fundamental question to be faced is this: "Was the time gained in speeding up legislation worth the disrespect for law and order which was created in the process?" Who is to judge?

Often civil disobedience has been maintained on the assumption that such action would have been justified in disobeying the laws of Hitler in Nazi Germany, or in rebelling against the sad misrepresentation of the colonies in England at the time of the revolution. But can anyone examine the record of the Congress, state legislatures, city ordinances, plus court actions during the scope of our national history and then justifiably make such a comparison? We do not live in a police state, this is not Nazi Germany, nor is this nation committed to a policy of misrepresentation such as that which occurred at the time of the Revolutionary War. Our history of less than two hundred years is an unprecedented commitment to justice, and this justice has been primarily grounded in our legal processes.

Which laws are we to obey? Until such time as someone can formulate a system for justice superior to that of our present juristic system, we are to obey *all* laws! There is no demand that we *like* every law passed by the legislative bodies of this nation. But there is a high demand—the highest demand, that of the biblical revelation—that we *obey* those laws.

The word INTEGRITY sums up the Ninth Commandment.

Notes

1. Brown, Driver, and Briggs, *A Hebrew and English Lexicon* (Oxford: Clarendon Press, 1952), p. 773.
2. *Ibid.*, p. 729.
3. R. H. Charles, *The Decalogue* (Edinburgh: T & T Clark, 1926), pp. 94 ff.
4. *Ibid.*, p. 99.

10
SECURITY

A man can find protection from theft and various other crimes against both his person and his property. But it is almost impossible to guarantee freedom from envy on the part of those with whom one lives in the community. Despite the difficulty of protecting members of a community from covetousness, freedom from envy is another right to which a person is entitled in the stable society. It is an *inalienable* right of every member within the covenant community.

"You shall not envy" (cf. Ex. 20:17; Deut. 5:21) is the tenth word of the Lord.

The significance of the biblical emphasis upon freedom from envy resides in the awareness that crimes against both one's person and one's property are more often than not born in feelings of greed and envy. It is highly significant that within the community of ancient Israel, members were entitled not only to the freedoms already discussed in commandments five through eight but to that intangible element of "freedom from envy" as well.

Sin represents man's refusal to accept his role as a created person by seeking to usurp the prerogatives of God and attempting to play the role in his own life which only God can play. Thus pride, whether intellectual, moral, or spiritual, lies at the heart of man's sinful rebellion.[1]

The Tenth Commandment is a reflection of this same quality

of pride, except that it is directed toward other men rather than toward God. The last commandment brings the reader face to face with the threat of a prideful interpretation of life in which he covets all that does not belong to him. Such a person has a self-exalted concept and feels justified in formulating some scheme whereby he can acquire that which belongs to another. He feels that his own desires are superior to the needs of others and his feelings of greed are more important than the rights of person and property on the part of others.

The Forms of the Commandment

Any investigation of the Tenth Commandment should take into consideration both the Exodus 20 and the Deuteronomy 5 rendering. While the meaning of the commandment is exactly the same in both accounts, the phrasing is distinctly reversed. The form in Exodus 20 will appear first.

Exodus places "house" as the first object of man's covetous desires, while Deuteronomy specifies "wife." "House," as used in Exodus, refers to the totality of one's family, including all one's possessions. The command could be paraphrased, "You shall not covet anything that is your neighbor's."

Having stated the all-inclusive term "house," Exodus then lists the possessions in their order of importance. Deuteronomy places woman in a category to herself. Then the all-inclusive term "house" is used, followed by the actual pieces of property —the field, servants, and animals (the order of importance for an ancient Hebrew). The "field" was not listed in the Exodus account. Its Deuteronomic inclusion *may* reflect a later time, after Israel had settled in the land. There would have been no great concern for a field in the desert. In following this pattern, Deuteronomy also may reflect a time when greater consideration for woman prevailed, resulting in the placing of woman in a separate category from other property.

The Exodus use of the verb "covet" refers to both "house"

and "wife" while Deuteronomy uses the verb "desire" with reference to "possessions."

Apart from the necessity of considering alternate readings in duplicate accounts of the Scripture, what may be learned from such a consideration? The essential message of God to his people remains unchanged, despite differences in wording. Obviously, in the form in which the commandments have come to us, there are variations. This does not adversely affect the positive command of God concerning the temptations which come to all of us. In fact, the variations should contribute to our understanding of the manner in which the Scriptures have come to us. It was not necessary that every word in a parallel account be dictated in exactly the same form for it to have authority. Neither the preservation of God's intention nor the authority of the Scriptures resides in the literal dictation or preservation of particular words. The Spirit of God is not so limited in conveying the eternal purposes of God.

Understanding the Commandment

The final commandment is unusual in that it deals with motivation, or inner desires, as opposed to outward action. S. R. Driver says in this regard that the commandment is "the most inward of all the commandments, forbidding not an external act but a hidden mental state, a state, however, which is the spring and root of nearly every sin against a neighbor, the unlawful *desire* for something which is another's." [2]

Intention of the command.—The word *chamadh*, translated "covet," actually means desire or to take pleasure in. It may reflect a perfectly legal action, indeed a commendable affection. The bad sense of the word can be determined only from the context. There are three basic usages of the word. In the bad sense the word means desire that is inordinate, ungoverned, selfish, or lustful (cf. Ex. 34:24; Deut. 7:24; Josh. 7:21; Micah 2:2; Prov. 6:25; 12:12). In addition, the word may mean "to take pleasure in" with reference to Israel's idolatrous tendencies (cf. Isa. 1:29; 44:9,11). Proverbs 1:22 states that "scoffers *delight* in scoffing." In the good sense the word is used of God (cf. Psalm 68:17). It is also used of the Suffering Servant: "No beauty that we should desire him" (Isa. 53:2).

Thus, whether or not it is evil to desire (the basic meaning of the word) must be decided in light of the action which it will likely precipitate and what the spirit of the desire does to the individual.

Exodus uses the word *'awah* to describe one's feelings toward a neighbor's house. Its basic meaning is much like that of "covet" and means incline or desire. It may refer to a king who desires to rule (cf. 2 Sam. 3:21; 1 Kings 11:37) or to so common an event as desiring food and drink (cf. Deut. 14:26).

Members of the covenant community are not to covet property belonging to another *with the view of taking that property*. It is not the biblical writer's intention to prohibit the desire for property as such but only to protect the right of one's neighbor to live with a feeling of security concerning his own possessions.

Scope of the commandment.—The use of the term "house" included the entire scope of a man's possessions. Although the word may mean "house" in the physical sense, quite often it is used of the entirety of one's family and possessions (cf. Gen. 12:17; 17:27; Lev. 17:3; Deut. 25:9–10).

It may well be that the commandment as originally given included the statement, "You shall not covet your neighbor's house," and that the latter part of the commandment was added as a commentary, specifying in detail that which was implied.

Motivation as an area of responsibility.—The motivational emphasis of the commandment is quite important and represents a significant degree of perception for early Israel. To understand that it is not only wrong to commit overt acts of injustice against society but that even to envision the acquisition of another's property is evil deals with the inner aspect of sin.

Robert I. Kahn has well expressed the importance of the last commandment:

> Next to the first, this is the most important of them all. The first commandment deals with foundations; the last with motivations. The first deals with the rock of ages; the last with the surging tides of desire. The first is an affirmation of the divine source of morality; the last deals with the wellsprings of immorality. The first implies that right thought will lead to right action; the last reminds us that wrong ideas will lead to wrong action.[3]

Admitted that the commandment does deal with motivation, however, there is considerable question concerning whether it should be interpreted solely in terms of inner attitude. The biblical writer, although this is unstated, quite likely had in mind *coveting* that led to the acquisition of another's property, not merely to evil desire in isolation from action. An interpretative translation, therefore, could be: "Do not covet with the deliberate intention of forcing from your neighbor his house, etc." The biblical writer more likely saw covetousness and illegal acquisition of property as the two sides of one's hand, one automatically accompanying the other.

Biblical understanding of covetousness.—The word "covet" and related words, such as coveted, coveting, covetous, covetousness, and covets, appear in only eight verses of the Old Testament.

Covetousness is systematically prohibited in the Old Testament, and refers to the "iniquity of his covetousness [with which] was I [God] angry" (Isa. 57:17). Apart from the prohibition within the Ten Commandments, men are spoken of as having coveted land (Mic. 2:2), gold, silver, and clothing (Josh. 7:21). The wicked man covets all day long (cf. Prov. 21:26), while the righteous man "covets many days, that he may enjoy good" (Psalm 34:12), a desire that is not condemned.

Jesus placed covetousness with evil thoughts, fornication,

theft, murder, adultery, wickedness, deceit, licentiousness, envy, slander, pride, and foolishness. He insisted that "these evil things come from within, and they defile a man" (Mark 7:23 f.). On one other occasion Jesus dealt with covetousness. In the preface to the parable of the rich fool, Jesus warned men to "take heed, and beware of all covetousness; for a man's life does not consist in the abundance of his possessions" (Luke 12:15).

Paul made reference to the Tenth Commandment (cf. Rom. 7:7; 13:9) and cited covetousness among those deeds of wickedness which characterize men who do not know God (cf. Rom. 1:29). He freely admitted that even in his own life "sin . . . wrought in me all kinds of covetousness" (Rom. 7:8). So reprehensible did he consider covetousness that he said that "covetousness must not even be named among you, as is fitting among saints" (Eph. 5:3). Toward the conclusion of his ministry he validated his ministry to the Ephesian elders by insisting that in the fulfilment of his apostleship and ministry among them, "I coveted no one's silver or gold or apparel" (Acts 20:33).

James explained wars and fightings among those to whom he wrote in terms of men who "covet and cannot obtain; so you fight and wage war" (James 4:2).

Despite all of these emphases, however, the seriousness of covetousness is nowhere so strongly emphasized as in Paul's apparent equation of covetousness with idolatry. Writing to the Colossians, he said, "Put to death therefore what is earthly in you: immorality, impurity, passion, evil desire, and covetousness, which is idolatry" (3:5). In speaking of individuals who were covetous, Paul warned the Ephesians; "Be sure of this, that no immoral or impure man, or one who is covetous (that is, an idolator), has any inheritance in the kingdom of Christ and of God" (5:5).

In what sense is covetousness synonymous with idolatry? The First Commandment deals with "no other gods." The Tenth Commandment deals with the inordinate desire for "things" which can eventually displace even God in one's life. Many a person has made a god of his possessions, giving to material goods his absolute devotion, even the total commitment of life. The identification of covetousness with idolatry should cause one to recognize the deeply serious nature of uncontrolled desire for material goods.

George Jackson suggests that one would have expected Jesus to say, "You cannot serve God and the world, or the devil." But he knew that there was a more deadly rival to the love and devotion to God—that of money. Therefore he said, "Ye cannot serve God and mammon" (Matt. 6:24). Paul, continues Jackson, "has the same tremendous contrast in his mind, when, writing to Timothy, he bids him, 'Charge them that are rich in this present world, that they be not high-minded, nor have their hope set on the uncertainty of riches, but on God.'" [4] Covetousness is one form of idolatry!

To Make Men Free Today

The LORD seeks to make men free today! The Commandments were not intended as restrictive burdens to enslave those who serve the living LORD of history. To the contrary, they were designed as the means whereby members of the covenant community could live in essential freedom with the LORD and with one another. Especially would the application of the Tenth Commandment make it possible for men to attain that freedom which the LORD intends for man to acquire. Envy and greed continue to stand among the more serious threats to the essential freedom of the human spirit.

What does the commandment have to contribute to life in the twentieth century?

First, *freedom from envy is an inalienable right of members within the covenant community.* If the people of God cannot be free from envy on the part of one another, where should such freedom be found? Yet, it is often true that among religious people, even among those who serve in leadership positions, envy and jealousy are more detrimental than among some groups who make no identification with the LORD.

We have not yet reached that high idealism of Paul, who said that when one "is honored, all rejoice together" (1 Cor. 12:26). Somehow, Paul's warning to the Galatians has a disturbing note of relevance about it for our own era. "If you bite and devour one another take heed that you are not consumed by one another" (Gal. 5:15). It is a sad day for the kingdom of God when members of the covenant community can be characterized by terms drawn from a dog fight—"bite and devour one another"!

Second, *the commandment clarifies the role of motivation as central to godly conduct.* The very consideration of covetousness in the context of the commandments which deal with murder, adultery, and theft should indicate the seriousness of motivation. Men within the covenant are to refrain from covetousness, not merely because of its detrimental effect on their own lives, but because motivation ultimately determines conduct. Just as one does not expect fresh water to flow from the ocean, neither should one expect purity of conduct to flow from seas of greed and envy.

To a great extent, every man eventually becomes like his thoughts. To conspire against a neighbor's wife, or his property, is hardly the type of motivation which produces godly conduct. Therefore, what you *think* may be even more important than what you *do.* Therefore, let us think thoughts of purity and godliness, putting away all feelings of covetousness, envy, greed, or lust.

Third, *envy and greed are directly related to one's absolute commitment.* There is a direct relationship between the first and the last of the commandments. Just as we are to have no commitment which transcends our commitment to the LORD, neither are we to be so consumed by our commitment to material goods as to *covet* that which belongs to our neighbor. While one could not prove that such covetousness transcends commitment to the Lord, it is highly probable that such is the case. Personal experience tends to confirm the assertion that those who are consumed by greed and envy for their neighbor's possessions, whether his wife or his property, are seldom those who have a sense of absolute commitment to the Lord. The reason for this is not hard to find. When one loves the Lord his God with all of his being, he will not spend the hours of the day or night scheming against his neighbor.

Fourth, *covetousness and envy reflect an essential failure to appreciate the rights of others.* Far too many assume that life was tailor-made for them and that others can make the best of whatever may be left. Such an inverted view of life, placing one's self on the top and others always on the bottom, fails to understand the nature of life within the community of faith. The welfare of the community was always of transcendent importance in the Old Testament (at times this even obscured the positive emphasis of individual rights and values). Biblical religion knows nothing of a life of unconcern for the welfare and better interests of one's brother. One seriously questions whether those who never appreciate another, whom they have seen, can appreciate God, whom they have not seen!

Fifth, *envy reflects an undue exaltation of self.* Just as it fails to appreciate the worth and significance of others, envy and covetousness unduly exalt the welfare and interests of the individual. Those who covet another's property manifest the conviction that supreme consideration should be given to their own selfish interests. When this attitude results in the overt appropriation of property, it is theft. When it results in a petulant and childish attitude on the part of many, even in the church, when they do not have their own way, it is immaturity. Both constitute a failure to embody the will of God in appraising one's own importance in the system of values within one's society. Although man inevitably begins with himself as the center in any given situation, this does not mean that such self-consideration is either divinely approved or representative of maturity on the part of the individual.

Sixth, *the morale of covenant people is especially likely to suffer from the detrimental effects of greed and envy*. Covetousness in churches and institutions of the church may never break forth into overt acts of theft against another person. Yet, its detrimental effects are felt. How tragic it is that the service of God is often so adversely affected by the selfishness of religious workers!

Seventh, *covetousness is an essential unwillingness to trust the Lord*. Over and over the Scriptures remind the people of God that the Lord will meet human need through his own processes as men cooperate with him. The Lord has placed us in a society in which physical needs can be met; dependent, of course, upon the manner in which those of us within the world community cooperate together. To reject the assurances of the Lord concerning his providential care and to "go it alone," by seeking to gain through covetous thought or deed that which we want, is to reject the way of faith. Covetousness is essentially a faithless attitude.

Eighth, *greed and covetousness are self-destructive to the individual, even when they do not produce overt action*. Like some corrosive acid within, envy eats away at the life center of the individual. As George Jackson has wisely observed:

> The penalty of the gold-heaper (is that) he gets his wealth at the cost of himself. Did you ever ponder that deep saying of the psalmist: "He gave them their request, but sent leanness into their soul"? Earth has not any sight so pitiful as that—the shrinking and shrivelling of a soul amid the piled-up splendours of material wealth.[5]

There are many, however, who never succeed in acquisition of hoped-for wealth who also are destroyed from within by the corruptive power of covetousness, greed, and envy.

Ninth, *freedom from envy is foundational to all other free-*

doms. This commandment, someone has said, contains "nine in one." There is a sense in which this assertion is true. Each of the successive commandments represents man's effort to project himself to a position of transcendence beyond the particular point of consideration within the commandment. In other words, man covets the property or the role described in each of the Commandments. He covets the role of God in his own life and implements his envy of God's role by usurping the prerogatives of God. He fails in other ways to acknowledge the absolute sovereignty of God. He denies to those with whom he is in community the essential freedoms which should characterize membership in the covenant community. The heart of man's denial of each of the Commandments, therefore, is his attitude of envy and greed which causes him to interpret all of life solely in terms of his own person and interests. Pride, expressed through envy or greed is at the heart of man's separation from the LORD.

The one word which characterizes best the Tenth Commandment is SECURITY. Every member of the covenant community has the right to freedom from the haunting threat that someone may implement his covetousness and violate the rights of person and property found in the Commandments. Covenant life ought to guarantee security to every person.

Notes

1. See Reinhold Niebuhr, *The Nature and Destiny of Man* (New York: Charles Scribner's Sons, 1949), pp. 178 ff.
2. S. R. Driver, *The Book of Exodus* (Cambridge: University Press, 1953), p. 200.
3. Robert I. Kahn, *The Ten Commandments for Today* (Garden City, New York: Doubleday & Co., Inc., 1964), p. 116. Copyright 1964 by Robert I. Kahn. Reprinted by permission of Doubleday & Co., Inc.
4. George Jackson, *The Ten Commandments* (Edinburgh: Anderson & Ferrier, 1898), pp. 182 ff.
5. *Ibid.*, p. 188.

BIBLIOGRAPHY

BERG, HAROLD EDWIN. *The Ten Commandments and You*. Philadelphia: Fortress Press, 1964.

BETTENSON, HENRY (ed.). *Documents of the Christian Church*. New York and London: Oxford University Press, 1947.

BOARDMAN, GEORGE DANA. *The Ten Commandments*. Philadelphia: Judson Press, 1946.

BRUNNER, EMIL. *The Divine Imperative*. Philadelphia: Westminster Press, 1947.

BURR, JOHN. *Studies on the Ten Commandments*. London: Allenson & Co., Ltd., 1935.

CARROLL, B. H. *The Ten Commandments*. Nashville: Broadman Press, 1938.

CHAPPEL, CLOVIS G. *Ten Rules for Living*. Nashville: Abingdon Press, 1938.

COFFIN, HENRY SLOAN. *The Ten Commandments*. New York: George H. Doran Co., 1915.

COFFMAN, JAMES BURTON. *The Ten Commandments Yesterday and Today*. Westwood, New Jersey: Fleming H. Revel Co., 1961.

DE VAUX, ROLAND. *Ancient Israel, Its Life and Institutions*. Translated by JOHN MCHUGH. New York: McGraw-Hill Book Co., Inc., 1961.

DYKES, J. OSWALD. *The Law of the Ten Words*. Hodder & Stoughton, New York: George H. Doran Co., 1884.

EICHRODT, WALTHER. *Theology of the Old Testament*. Translated by J. A. BAKER. Vol. I. Philadelphia: Westminster Press, 1961.

ELDER, HUGH. *The Laws of Life*. Edinburgh: Published for the Church of Scotland, Committee on the Religious Instruction of Youth by the Publications Committee.

FARRAR, FREDERIC W. *The Voice from Sinai*. London: Isbister and Co., Ltd., 1896.

FINLAY, TERENCE J. *The Ten Commandments.* New York: Charles Scribner's Sons, 1961.
FORD, W. HERSCHEL. *Simple Sermons on the Ten Commandments.* Grand Rapids: Zondervan Publishing House, 1956.
FORELL, GEORGE W. *Ethics of Decision.* Philadelphia: Muhlenberg Press, 1955.
FOX, EMMET. *The Ten Commandments the Master Key to Life.* New York: Harper & Bros., 1953.
GINEVER, VIOLET. *The Twelve Commandments.* London: S.P.C.K., 1962.
HOOKE, S. H. *Babylonian and Assyrian Religion.* London: Hutchinson House, 1953.
HOOPER, JOHN. *Early Writings of John Hooper, Lord Bishop of Gloucester and Worcester.* Cambridge: University Press, 1843.
JACKSON, GEORGE. *The Ten Commandments.* Edinburgh and London: Anderson & Ferrier, 1898.
KAHN, ROBERT I. *The Ten Commandments for Today.* Garden City, New York: Doubleday & Co., Inc., 1964.
KENNETT, R. H. *Deuteronomy and the Decalogue.* Cambridge: University Press, 1920.
KUIPER, HENRY J. (ed.). *Sermons on the Ten Commandments.* Grand Rapids: Zondervan Publishing House, 1951.
LASSERRE, JEAN. *War and the Gospel.* Translated by OLIVER COBURN. London: James Clarke & Co., Ltd., 1962.
MARTY, MARTIN E. *The Hidden Discipline.* St. Louis: Concordia Publishing House, 1962.
MASSEE, J. C. *The Gospel in the Ten Commandments.* Butler, Indiana: Higley Press, n.d.
MCCARTHY, JOHN CANON. *Problems in Theology.* Westminster, Maryland: Newman Press, 1960.
MENDENHALL, GEORGE E. *Law and Covenant in Israel and the Ancient Near East.* Pittsburgh: The Biblical Colloquium, 1955.
MORGAN, G. CAMPBELL. *The Ten Commandments.* Chicago: Bible Institute Colportage Association of Chicago, 1901.
MYERS, SYDNEY. *The Ten Words.* London: Independent Press, 1956.
NELSON, C. ELLIS. *Love and the Law.* Richmond, Virginia: John Knox Press, 1963.
NIEDERMEYER, FREDERICK DAVID. *The Ten Commandments Today.* Boston: Stratford Co., 1928.
NOTH, MARTIN. *Exodus.* London: SCM Press, Ltd., 1962.
OLDHAM, J. H. *Life Is Commitment.* London: SCM Press, Ltd., 1953.

PEDERSEN, JOHANNES. *Israel, Its Life and Culture.* 4 vols. London: Oxford University Press, 1947.

REIK, THEODOR. *Mystery on the Mountain.* New York: Harper & Bros., 1959.

ROWLEY, HAROLD H. *Moses and the Decalogue.* Manchester: Manchester University Press, 1951.

ROWLEY, H. H. *The Rediscovery of the Old Testament.* Philadelphia: Westminster Press, 1946.

SCHULLER, ROBERT. *God's Way to the Good Life.* Grand Rapids: William B. Eerdmans Publishing Co., 1963.

SETON, ERNEST THOMPSON. *The Natural History of the Ten Commandments.* New York: Charles Scribner's Sons, 1907.

SLEMP, JOHN CALVIN. *Twelve Laws of Life.* Philadelphia: Judson Press, 1950.

VON RAD, GERHARD. *Old Testament Theology.* Vol. I. Edinburgh and London: Oliver & Boyd, 1962.

WATSON, THOMAS. *The Ten Commandments.* London: The Banner of Truth Trust, 1959. U. S. Distributors, Christian Literature Crusade, Fort Washington, Pa.

WEATHERLY, OWEN M. *The Ten Commandments in Modern Perspective.* Richmond: John Knox Press, 1961.